YORK NOTES

General Editors: Professor A.N. Jeffares (*University of Stirling*) & Professor Suheil Bushrui (*American University of Beirut*)

Edmund Spenser

THE FAERIE QUEENE

BOOK I

Notes by Robert Welch

MA (NUI) PH D (LEEDS)
Lecturer, School of English, University of Leeds

YORK PRESS
Immeuble Esseily, Place Riad Solh, Beirut.

LONGMAN GROUP LIMITED
Longman House,
Burnt Mill,
Harlow,
Essex

First published 1985
ISBN 0 582 79235 5
Printed in Hong Kong by
Sing Cheong Printing Press Ltd

Contents

Part 1: Introduction *page* 5
The life of Edmund Spenser 5
The religious and political background to Book I of *The Faerie Queene* 10
A note on the text 15

Part 2: Summaries 17
A general summary 17
Detailed summaries 17

Part 3: Commentary 43
Kind 43
Allegory 44
Sources 46
The moral allegory and the narrative 47
The quest for Holinesse 56
The other figures in the story 56
Structure 62
The Spenserian stanza and Spenser's language 64

Part 4: Hints for study 67
Points for detailed study 67
Useful quotations 70
Arrangement of material 72
Specimen questions 72
Specimen answer 73
Suggested outlines for other answers 75

Part 5: Suggestions for further reading 76

The author of these notes 78

Part 1

Introduction

The life of Edmund Spenser

Unlike Shakespeare, the only writer of the English Renaissance greater than the subject of these Notes, we do know a good deal about Spenser. For much of his life he was a public official in Ireland, which means that records of his activities survive in state documents.

He was born in about 1552 of a merchant family in London. He attended the Merchant Taylor School there, one of the recently founded grammar schools, the headmaster of which was Richard Mulcaster (*c.*1530-1611). Mulcaster was a stern idealist and Puritan (the Puritans were opposed to the Church of Rome, for what they regarded as its worldly abuses); but as a teacher he encouraged his charges to think and express themselves as individuals. He put on plays at Court every year so that his boys would learn discipline and 'audacity'. The classics were taught at the Merchant Taylor School, but English was not neglected and attention was drawn to old and regional words, an interest we see at work in Spenser's writing. The boys were not just made to think about translating a text or establishing the meaning of its parts; their attention was also directed towards the narrative, argument, and meaning of the works they studied.

In 1569, when he was seventeen, Spenser contributed to a work of Protestant propaganda compiled by a refugee from the Low Countries (then under the control of Catholic Spain) called Jan van der Noot. The work is entitled *A Theatre for Worldlings*, and is an attack on the abuses, worldliness, and idolatry of the Roman Catholic Church. It comprised poems selected from such writers as the Italian Petrarch (1304-74) and the French Joachim du Bellay (1522-60), a prose commentary by Van der Noot interpreting the poems, and engravings further emphasising the ways in which the propagandist wished the poems to be read. Spenser translated the poetry into English verse. Straightaway, at the very outset of his career, Spenser had involved himself in religious controversy; he had made contact with great European writers (though in a somewhat limiting context); and had brought pictures and poetry together. In his own work the emblematic method, as it is called, was later to be much in evidence. With the emblematic method the poet sets out, quite deliberately, to build up a picture in the reader's mind. As the picture is being assembled the writer also supplies the interpretation he wishes the reader to put on it so that a moral intention is emphasised and realised by the reader himself, as he participates in the construction of the mental picture which the poet has devised. This is how Spencer's allegory works, and already, even before he went to university, in his collaboration with the Puritan Van der Noot, he had stumbled upon the essentials of the method.

Cambridge, Spenser's University, was in his time a place much agitated by controversy. John Whitgift (*c.* 1530-1604), Master of Trinity College, was a supporter of Queen Elizabeth I's attempt to secure a Church of England, free from Rome, while avoiding the more radical reforms for which some Puritans were calling. Thomas Cartwright (1535-1603), however, of St John's College, looked for the abolition of all authority not based upon Scripture. Whitgift later became Archbishop of Canterbury, while Cartwright was relieved of his Professorship of Divinity.

Spenser received his B.A. in 1573. While an undergraduate he became a friend of Gabriel Harvey (*c.* 1550-1630), a fellow of his College, Pembroke, with whom he exchanged ideas on literature and religion. In 1576 he graduated as M.A. and during these years he seems to have fallen in love with a girl, whom he calls 'Rosalind' in *The Shepheardes Calendar* (1579).

Although he always maintained that the Spencers of Althorp in Northamptonshire (a very old aristocratic family) were distant relations, Spenser was without any special advantages of birth or fortune. He was dependent on the goodwill of others for his livelihood: in Elizabethan England merit, ability, even genius were in themselves no guarantee of success. When Dr John Young, Master of Pembroke, was made Bishop of Rochester, he appointed Spenser as his secretary in 1578.

In 1579 Spenser married Machabyas Chylde, and in December of the year *The Shepheardes Calendar* appeared, dedicated to Sir Philip Sidney (1554-86). Spenser was on the fringe of the poetic and philosophical circle that surrounded Sidney, among whom were Fulke Greville (1554-1628) and Sir Edward Dyer (*c.* 1545-1607): he said they had him 'in some use of familiarity'. He also received some notice from Robert Dudley, Earl of Leicester (1532-88), a great favourite of the Queen, who was also part of the Sidney group and a patron of poets.

Possibly through Sidney's influence, in 1580 Spenser was made secretary to Lord Grey de Wilton, the newly appointed Lord Governor of Ireland. Sidney's own father, Sir Henry Sidney, had held the same difficult appointment. In Dublin Spenser became a friend of Lodowick Bryskett (*c.* 1545-1612) who was Clerk to the Council there. He took up residence in New Abbey in County Kildare, a property confiscated from Catholic friars with the dissolution of the monasteries brought about by Henry VIII. All the time he was at work on *The Faerie Queene*.

Being secretary to the Lord Governor meant that Spenser saw Ireland and its inhabitants at first hand. For the Elizabethans Ireland was a savage country: its bogs and wildernesses, its terrible empty winters, its continual rainfall, meant the ruin of many an English reputation. The Irish, always renowned as fierce fighters, began, in the sixteenth century, to think of themselves as champions of Catholicism, fighting a Holy War for the sake of the true Church against English Protestantism. The Pope, Gregory XIII, was eager to subjugate what he regarded as the heretical power of England, and was sympathetic to those among the Irish who came to seek his aid in influencing France and Spain to assist them in their struggle against Tudor England. Eventually, in 1580, a small force of Spaniards landed at Smerwick in County Kerry, at a place which they called Fort del Oro. Grey marched on them and quickly defeated the Spaniards, insisting that they surrender unconditionally. The massacre of the soldiers in the fort, and the details of the execution of the servant of the Papal ambassador, Nicholas Sanders (his legs were broken, then he was hung from the walls of the fort), imprinted themselves on Spenser's mind.

Years later, in his prose treatise, *A View of the Present State of Ireland* (written 1596, not published until 1633), Spenser defended the ferocity of Grey's action on the grounds that, by behaving cruelly on that occasion, the English were giving notice of their single-mindedness in suppressing insurrection and in resisting invasion.

While Elizabeth was pleased with Grey's handling of the affair at Smerwick, she grew uneasy with his uncompromising manner in dealing with the Irish. Grey believed in rewarding those working under him in the Irish administration with gifts of lands confiscated from the Irish rebels (among the recipients was Spenser: that was how he acquired New Abbey), and the Queen heard of this from officials, who, unrewarded themselves, pointed out to her that income which could be hers was being passed on to Grey's friends. Grey's reiterated pleas to be recalled were heeded and he left Ireland in August 1582. Spenser called him 'the pillar of my life' in a dedicatory sonnet to *The Faerie Queene*.

The new Lord Deputy of Ireland was Sir John Perrot. Spenser's friend, Lodowick Bryskett, became Clerk to the Council of Munster, and he appointed Spenser as his deputy, which meant that Spenser discharged most of the duties of the post. The President of Munster was Sir John Norris, later succeeded by his brother Thomas. Gerald Fitzgerald, Earl of Desmond, in open rebellion since 1579, had eluded capture until 1583 when he was killed near Tralee in County Kerry.

Government forces and rebels had, between them, made Munster a desert, so that, in the words of the Gaelic chronicle, *The Four Masters*, 'The lowing of a cow, or the voice of a ploughman, could scarcely be heard from Dunquin to Cashel'. Famine, disease and war had all taken their toll. Now, with the Earl dead, in spite of the threat of Spanish invasion (the numerous harbours of the south-west seaboard were an open invitation to this), was the time to re-settle Munster, to replant and rebuild.

Plantation was the solution: the land would be surveyed and valued; English settlers would move in, and would *undertake* to build a house and re-cultivate the land, gradually bringing order, peace and prosperity. Spenser himself was involved in the inspections that preceded the plantation, and he became an undertaker (settler on forfeited land) at Kilcolman in County Cork, on lands adjoining the extensive estate of Sir Thomas Norris at Mallow. This was in 1588, the year of the defeat of the Spanish Armada.

By now parts of *The Faerie Queene* were circulating in manuscript in London. Sir Walter Raleigh visited Spenser at Kilcolman in 1589 and persuaded him to go to London with him to present *The Faerie Queene* to the woman around whom the entire poem revolves, Elizabeth I herself. In 1590 William Ponsonby, a bookseller in St Paul's Churchyard, published the first three books which Spenser dedicated to the Queen. She awarded him a pension of fifty pounds a year.

In 1591, after a brief return to Ireland, Spenser published a volume entitled *Complaints*, containing elegies, satires and philosophical reflections on the ruins of time. But the strain and falsity of court life did not agree with him. Devoted as he was to the Queen, he found the place-hunting and the readiness to abandon self-respect, which her supreme authority and power produced, distasteful. This is evident in *Colin Clout's Come Home Againe*, a poem published in 1591, which tells the story of his journey to England with Raleigh; the reception of *The Faerie Queene* at court; his experiences there; and his glad return to Ireland, leaving behind the anxiety and pressure of trying to gain notice from the great and powerful. It seems he thought that William Cecil, Lord Burghley (1520-98), the Lord Chancellor, had blocked his advancement. At any rate, he was back in Ireland in 1592.

Spenser's first wife had died some time earlier, possibly before he left Ireland. He had two children by her: a son, Sylvanus; and a daughter, Katherine. Probably in 1594 he married in Cork City Elizabeth Boyle, an English girl from Northamptonshire. His courtship of her is described in a sonnet sequence, the *Amoretti*, which records both the physical and the spiritual awakening of love (the two are never far apart in Spenser). The conclusion of the *Amoretti* is a long marriage poem, the *Epithalamion*, one of the most formally perfect poems in English, and one of the most joyous. Both poems were printed in London in 1595, by Ponsonby.

In 1596 Spenser was again in England, seeing to the publication of the next three books of *The Faerie Queene*, with Ponsonby again the publisher. The second edition of Books I-III, reset from the edition of 1590, came out at the same time.

By now Hugh O'Neill, Earl of Tyrone (1540-1616), had been declared a traitor and had assumed the hereditary Irish title of 'The O'Neill'. Within a few weeks he submitted again, but this was merely to gain time so that he could improve his contacts with Spain. There were rumours that a second Armada was being equipped. By 1596, against the background of this uncertainty, with O'Neill exercising all his statecraft in order to co-ordinate Irish resentment against the English, Spenser completed his *View of the Present State of Ireland*. Here he described the causes of Irish discontent (as he saw them) and put forward proposals for dealing with them. His view is that the Irish should be treated severely; the rebels should be rooted out and executed without mercy; and English culture and the English language should be established. A Lord Lieutenant should be appointed to look after Irish interests, protecting them from unwarranted interference by the English Government. Above all he is against wavering and indecision in crown policy.

Also in 1596, Spenser's *Fowre Hymnes*—to Love and to Heavenly Love, to Beauty and to Heavenly Beauty—were published. They show Spenser reconciling the Platonic ideas of love and beauty (in which they are seen as the essential form of life itself), with the Christian ideals of charity and devotion.

Returning to Ireland he found the situation to be more or less as he had described it in the *View*, where 'all have their ears upright' waiting for the word to break into rebellion. O'Neill's hostility finally came into the open in June 1598, when he laid siege to a ford on the river Blackwater in Ulster. The Battle of the Yellow Ford followed, in which Sir Henry Bagenal, Marshal of the English army, was shot. Seven years before O'Neill had eloped with Bagenal's sister, Mabel. An intelligence and propaganda network, organised by O'Neill, spread throughout the country, inciting the Irish Catholics, promising them the return of their old lands, and pledging too the re-establishment of the Roman Catholic faith with the defeat and expulsion of the English. Munster was not exempt. One of O'Neill's men in Munster was a Captain Richard Tyrell, an Englishman who had 'gone native'. He led insurgents from Leinster into Munster. Many of the Irish immediately joined them, out of sympathy, or simply because they did not wish their lands despoiled. Most of the 'undertakers', knowing that their own tenants would go over to the rebels, fled to the safety of Cork or the other towns. Spenser with his wife and children did the same. His house at Kilcolman was destroyed.

Around this time Spenser was made Sheriff of Cork, an office he did not live to enjoy. He left Cork in December, bearing letters from Sir Thomas Norris, Lord President of Munster, for the privy council in Whitehall. In January 1599 he died in Westminster.

In 1609 the two cantos of Mutabilitie appeared, from the Book of Constancy, Book VII of *The Faerie Queene* in the first folio of that work. Their setting is the countryside around Kilcolman.

The religious and political background to Book I of *The Faerie Queene*

Spencer's intention throughout this poem, as he told Walter Raleigh in the letter included with the 1590 edition of the first three books, was 'to fashion a gentleman or noble person'. This cannot be emphasised too much. Nowadays we are not accustomed to thinking of poems as having direct or immediate effects on our moral life and our general behaviour, but this was by no means the case in other periods of history. Spenser certainly wished to have an effect on the reader, and a good one. If we take the word 'fashion' from the above quotation we may be able to gain some idea of his purpose. Fashioning here means shaping or moulding: he would wish the reading of his poem to make a new kind of man. As the Word of God made all created things, so the words of the poet, shaped and fashioned by metre, deepened by reflection and thought, would bring into being a new, independent kind of man, responsive to Holinesse and free of Error, duplicity (Duessa) and the fearsome tyranny of the Old Dragon in all his forms. Spenser wanted, in other words, to write a Protestant poem, which would show the individual spirit in its quest for truth (Una), fighting against the false delusive worldliness of Catholicism (represented in Lucifera), and its proud willingness to imprison the conscience of its members (the giant Orgoglio's dungeon).

The Faerie Queene, then, is a Protestant poem, and a product of the Reformation. The Reformation of the sixteenth century wished to bring about a reform in the doctrine and practices of the Church of Rome, but eventually it led to the founding of the different Protestant churches. The leaders of this movement were Martin Luther (1483-1546), Ulrich Zwingli (1484-1531), and John Calvin (1509-64).

Henry VIII (The Lion)

During the reign of Elizabeth's father, Henry VIII, the Reformation came to England. The Reformers, or Protestants, wanted to create a new kind of church and a new kind of man, one who would strengthen his faith through personal reflection on the Bible, and who would reject the claims that the Church of Rome made to sole authority in matters of faith and morals. They also opposed the emphasis that the Roman Catholic Church placed on ritual: during the time of Henry VIII a zealous lawyer raised up a dog in church as the priest elevated the host at the consecration of the Mass.* Transubstantiation, in which Catholics believed, whereby the bread on the altar becomes the body of Christ, was, by the more extreme reformers, mocked at as superstition, 'hocus-pocus' (which comes from the Latin words—Hic Est Enim Corpus—which the priest says over the bread: 'For this is my body'). Henry, it should be said, resisted the worst extremes of zeal among the Protestants, but he himself, from 1527 onwards, had reason to wish for the dissolution of the link with Rome. He wanted to put aside his wife, Catherine of Aragon, and marry Anne Boleyn, who, he was sure, would provide him with an heir. Unfortunately Catherine was the aunt of the Holy Roman Emperor, Charles V, who had 'the pope in his pocket'.†

In 1533 Anne was pregnant with Henry's child; the marriage with Catherine was declared invalid, in England at least; and Henry and Anne were married. The King was excommunicated by Rome and in 1534 the Church of England was declared independent of Rome. The child for which this break took place was not, as everyone had hoped, a boy, but a girl, Elizabeth herself, the dominant figure in Spenser's poem. The lion in Book I is Henry.

Edward VI

Anne Boleyn was executed and her successor, Jane Seymour, gave birth to a son, Edward, who became Henry's successor when the king died in 1547. Even though Henry opposed the tendency among the more radical reformers to interpret the Bible for themselves, he nevertheless entrusted the tuition of Edward to men sympathetic to reform. During his reign, in 1549, Thomas Cranmer, Archbishop of Canterbury (1489-1556), introduced *The Book of Common Prayer*, which took a middle way, in that it incorporated many traditional elements in the ritual while suppressing some that the Protestants found offensive. Furthermore, it was in English, thereby greatly reducing the element of mystery which surrounded the Latin liturgy. From Geneva Calvin urged the boy-king and his advisers to root out the 'relics of popery'. In 1550 all the altars were removed from the London churches.

*J. R. Green, *A Short History of the English People*, Macmillan, London, 1876, p.346.
†S. T. Bindoff, *Tudor England*, Penguin Books, Harmondsworth, 1966, p.84.

Mary Tudor (Duessa)

Edward died in 1553 and Mary Tudor, daughter of Catherine of Aragon, assumed the throne. Her ambition was to renew the links with Rome, which she did within six months. Many Protestants fled abroad, to the centres of radical thought (Geneva, Basle), awaiting the day when the Church of England would again be liberated from what they saw as the tyranny of popery. While at Geneva some of these refugees worked on the translation of the Bible known as The Geneva Bible (1560), which had a marginal commentary much used by the Puritans. It is quite clear that this was the version of the Bible that Spenser had most often before him.

During Mary's reign all the reforms introduced during Edward's were revoked. The Latin Mass, with all the pomp of the Roman rite, was soon being said in the London churches, from which, not long before, the altars themselves had been removed.

Mary was negotiating a marriage treaty with Philip of Spain, a member of the house of Habsburg, headed by the Holy Roman Emperor Charles V. Despite a rising in Kent, led by Sir Thomas Wyatt (1503-42), in opposition to the alliance with Spain and Rome, Philip and Mary were married in 1554 in Winchester Cathedral. These two figure as Duessa and Orgoglio in Book I of *The Faerie Queene*.

Mary began to persecute heretics: the first martyr of her reign was John Rogers, burnt at the stake in Smithfield in 1555; and before 'bloody' Mary died, some three hundred people were executed. The fiery Protestant and idealist, Hugh Latimer (1485-1555), once bishop of Chichester, who had thrown the statue of the Virgin Mary out of the Cathedral church, was arrested and burnt at the stake; so, too, was Nicholas Ridley (1500-55), who had removed the altars from the churches in London.

Henry VIII's break with Rome had been a political expedient, but it also reflected a very strong trend in popular feeling at the time, to which men like Latimer gave voice. Mary enjoyed a certain amount of popularity on her accession: there was still a regard for the old religion; but this soon disappeared when she made the alliance with Spain. When she began executing Protestants many were appalled and disgusted. Her fiery ardour for the sake of the True Church, as she regarded it, meant that her memory was reviled by many Englishmen for a long time. Her policies, too, meant that the Roman Church became associated with duplicity, betrayal, sensuality, and cruelty, all qualities we see represented in the figure of Duessa. Duessa's appearance in Spenser is alluring, but underneath her exterior finery she is ugly, a sterile, disgusting, loathsome hag. Una, on the other hand is simple Truth, one and undivided, loyal and gentle. She is the true Church of England (just as Duessa is Roman Catholicism) and she is also, in certain respects, Elizabeth, who, according to Spenser, delivered England from the terror, oppression and sterility of Mary's reign. That the Faerie Queene herself is Elizabeth also need not trouble us too much, as Spenser's allegorical figures are polyvalent: that is, they can assume a number of different significances at the same time, giving a cluster of meanings, in which the reader is expected to discover coherence. In that discovery he will be 'fashioning' his mind in perceiving the truth for himself, a thoroughly Protestant form of discipline, whereby reading becomes a spiritual exercise.

Elizabeth (Gloriana: Una)

Elizabeth, then, was seen as the deliverer, and her accession in 1558 was thought of as instituting a period of religious and intellectual freedom and self-expression. She was her father's daughter: forceful, enigmatic, shrewd. Physically vain, she was also intellectually formidable, knowing French and Italian as well as Latin and some Greek. In religion she was a moderate, but she did not attempt to give Mary's Catholicism a more human face. Instead she opted for a Protestantism which removed Papal Supremacy (re-instituted in Mary's reign) and returned the headship of the Church of England to the monarch. The English *Book of Common Prayer* of Thomas Cranmer was also brought back into use, in doing which she appealed to the pride her people took in their Englishness, and honoured the loyalty and integrity of Cranmer himself, who, during Mary's persecution, scorned to seek refuge in Geneva or Basle, thereby obliging her ministers to execute him.

In 1570 Elizabeth was excommunicated by Pope Pius V, as her father had been, and her subjects were absolved by the Pope from their allegiance to the queen. This, however, only served to strengthen the feelings of loyalty most of her people had for her, though it made Elizabeth very aware of the forces acting on men's minds that can create division and discord. Throughout her reign she displayed a hatred of subversion and civil disobedience, and her poets and dramatists shared this horror, though with them it often extended into fascination with civil strife and religious and political instability. Spenser and William Shakespeare (1564-1616) are two writers preoccupied with concord and discord. This, in the end, is their single most pervasive theme; both of them see the Queen as embodying concord. Spenser, the Puritan, sees discord as Satan, manifesting himself on earth as the Dragon of the old religion, the beast of Revelation, whose nature is to spread error, deception and despair wherever he goes, that men's souls may be ruined, and that they may lose sight of their innate Holinesse.

The cruelty and tyranny of the Catholic Church was symbolised, for Protestants, in the St Bartholomew's Day Massacre of 24 August 1572, in which some twelve thousand French Protestants, Huguenots, were slaughtered in Paris and in the rest of France.

Philip II of Spain, with whom Elizabeth had maintained an uneasy peace, turned against her when she supported the rebel provinces of the Low Countries, which were under Spanish rule. In 1585 the Spanish ambassador in Rome laid before the Pope plans for the project which was to become the Spanish Armada. This would be a Catholic invasion of a heretical country presided over by an excommunicated Queen. It failed. English seamanship and the English weather contrived to sink the huge force of ships.

We have seen that in 1580 Philip sent a Spanish force to the south-west of Ireland, to assist the Desmond rebellion in Munster which was defeated by Lord Grey. In the 1590s he supported the Tyrone rebellion, and in 1596 sent ten thousand men to O'Neill's aid. But this expedition was dispersed by gales as soon as it set out. In 1597 further help was forthcoming, but it too achieved little, and in the next year Philip died.

In the sixteenth century, then, religion was politics and politics was religion. Protestantism and Catholicism were locked in sectarian struggle, not just for the men's souls, but for their bodies as well. Elizabeth, a Protestant virgin Queen, tried, in England, to steer a middle course between the extremes of Catholic ardour and Puritan zeal. Her aim was stability, settlement, independence, and the prosperity of her country. She was genuinely attached to her people and wished for their well-being and peace. This she felt was threatened by the forces of discord that were continually escaping from the Pandora's box of religious controversy. Her object was concord.

Spenser, the poet who, more than any other in the Elizabethan age, wrote of this concord, and located it, to a large extent, in the person and energy of the Virgin Queen herself, was a man of Puritan inclinations. If we think of Puritanism as Calvinism only, with its stern doctrine of the Elect (those chosen by God to be saved) and the damned (those predestined never to have access to grace), then we can gain no insight into Spenser's frame of mind. But if we think of Puritanism in a more kindly light, as an attitude towards the Christian life in which one may become one of the Elect through discipline of mind and soul, then we can see it as a more radical form of Protestantism, with greater emphasis on individual effort, thought, and prayer than had been common in orthodox Catholicism for some time. It was this form of Puritanism that became translated to America with the founding Fathers, and it still holds a deep attraction for many Americans, reconciling, as it can do, hard work for gain with sanctity.

Mention of America brings us back to Spenser and Elizabeth, because one of Spenser's aims was to write an Imperial poem (as Virgil (70-19BC), the Latin epic poet had done for Rome), in which Elizabeth would be the Empress who would establish on earth an Empire of modesty, tolerance, peace and unity (Una). Truth for Spenser as Puritan and Platonist,* was one, and the Queen, ideally, was the bringer of concord, union, and peace. She was single (unmarried), virgin, and chaste, and would set aside all duplicity and trouble through her knights. In Book I her knight is Holinesse, and he embodies England, the source from which the Empire of peace was to spread out, stretching as far, even, as the Americas, and, needless to say, including Ireland, that savage place and stumbling block to Elizabethan expansion, which Spenser knew so well. Holinesse is St George, and his name means the ploughman who ploughs the earth of England itself, which, under the care of Gloriana, the Faerie Queene, will bring forth fruit a hundredfold. All this will come about through the unity of truth (Una) to which Elizabeth I is seen to bear witness.

We see here the idealising force of Spenser's mind. What he looked for was the sanctifying of the whole nation, and his poem should, he thought, work towards this by exercising the minds of his readers in 'vertuous and gentle discipline'. This discipline would then be an armour against the unholy forces of false faith, sensuality and despair, into which Catholicism led the unconscious and uninformed mind. Spenser's poem seeks to answer every aspect of the political and religious debate of the time in English and Protestant terms.

A note on the text

To our knowledge, no manuscripts or drafts of *The Faerie Queene* survive. Spenser's friend at Cambridge, Gabriel Harvey, had seen some part of it in manuscript in 1580; and Lodowick Bryskett saw 'parcels' of it in Dublin, where it circulated before publication in the 1580s. In 1588, Abraham Fraunce, a dramatist and rhetorician, had seen part of Book II in something like its final form, because he quotes from it, citing the numbers of canto and stanza that obtained in the 1590 printed edition. Christopher Marlowe (1564-93) imitated I.vii. 32 in *Tamburlaine*, Part II, which was written probably around 1587.

Spenser saw a good deal of his work through the press, so that we can be sure that we have his work much as he would have wished us to have

*Platonism is an idealistic philosophy deriving from the works of Plato who lived (427-347BC) in Athens.

it, something we cannot say of Shakespeare's work, for example, as he showed remarkably little anxiety to have his drama printed. But even among his fellow poets Spenser is something of an exception in showing such a keen interest in publication: the works of Sir Philip Sidney and Sir Walter Raleigh were not published until long after their deaths. The reason for this may be found, to some extent, in Spenser's less exalted origins; and in the fact that he was much more of a moralist and a propagandist than the other two, and sought a wide audience for his poem of Empire and Virtue.

The first three books appeared in 1590, along with the letter to Raleigh, explaining the allegorical method used. In 1596 Books IV-VI were added, and the letter dropped, possibly because Raleigh was out of favour with the Queen. A folio edition of the entire poem as we have it now, along with the two cantos of Mutabilitie, appeared in 1609. To the 1609 compiler these two final cantos seem part of a seventh Book of Constancy.

Collected works appeared in 1611, 1617 and 1679. In 1758 an annotated edition appeared with a very useful commentary by J. Upton. *The Faerie Queene*, edited by J. C. Smith, was published by the Clarendon Press, Oxford, in 1909, and this formed part of the *Poetical Works of Spenser* in the Oxford University Press edition of 1912, edited by Ernest de Selincourt and J. C. Smith. This brings us up to modern editions of the poem, for which see the first section of Part 5.

There are scholars who dream about uncovering a lost manuscript of *The Faerie Queene* in some forgotten corner of a library, in Dublin or Cork or Kent or London; somewhere there may be a cache containing Books VII to XII of Spenser's massive project, but we have to admit that this seems unlikely. What we have of *The Faerie Queene* now is probably all that Spenser wrote, and it may well be complete in itself.

Part 2

Summaries

of Book I of THE FAERIE QUEENE

A general summary

The Red Crosse Knight, the champion of Una (Truth), sets out to defeat the Dragon that holds her parents in captivity in Eden. He defeats Error but is deceived by Archimago and leaves Una. He is further led astray by Duessa. In her company he goes to the House of Pride, and falls captive to the monster Orgoglio. While separated from her Knight, Una is protected by a lion and by Sir Satyrane. Though freed by Arthur, the Red Crosse Knight is still weak and succumbs to despair. Una brings him to the House of Holinesse, where he is made whole and granted a vision of the Eternal City, Heaven itself. Thus fortified, he defeats the Dragon and is betrothed to Una.

Detailed summaries

In a letter to Sir Walter Raleigh, on 23 January 1589, Spenser makes several points about his allegorical epic, *The Faerie Queene*:

1. His poem is to comprise twelve books (of which six and part of the seventh survive).
2. The poem is an allegory or a 'darke conceit'. An allegory is a story in which meanings, at first hidden in 'darknesse', come to light in the reader's mind, through the artistry of the story-telling.
3. The purpose of his poem is very definite: he wishes to improve virtue and 'gentle' discipline in his readers.
4. Arthur, familiar from British tradition, is to embody all the twelve moral virtues, each of which will have a book to itself.
5. The Faerie Queene is Glory, Gloriana, whom he partly identifies with Elizabeth I, Queen of England.
6. Gloriana is the object of Arthur's quest.
7. Book XII (which we do not have) was to bring all the stories together. It was to describe the annual feast of the Faerie Queene, which took twelve days, on each of which one of the knights was to tell his story, until the full moral significance of the twelve would be revealed in the coming of Arthur to the court of Faerie Land. Arthur intervenes in all the books, and Book XII was to be the expression of his virtue, Magnificence (generosity, glory, authority).

8. Book I opens with the legend of the Red Crosse Knight who represents the virtue of Holiness. In this book we meet him right in the "middest" of the action when he is already on his quest. In Book XII, had it been written, we should have heard how at the Faerie Queene's feast 'a tall clownishe young man' throws himself at her feet seeking favour. A lady comes in riding a white ass, and tells the company that her father and mother have, for many years, been kept under siege in a brass castle by a huge dragon. The clumsy knight offers himself as her champion: the lady says that she will accept him only if the armour she has with her fits him, which it does, perfectly, so that he is the 'goodliest' knight in the hall, the true champion of Holinesse.

Book I: Proem

In the first four stanzas Spenser, in the traditional manner of the epic poet, calls upon the muses to inspire him. These are: the muse of history (Clio); Venus with her son Cupid in benign aspect (he is asked to leave the 'Heben bow' apart); and Elizabeth I herself, the mirror of divine grace. Her light, like that of her Isle, Britain, shines throughout the world, like Phoebus, the sun god. This, we are given to understand, is to be a work of devotion, improvement, and praise of Britain.

NOTES AND GLOSSARY:

whilome: once, some time before

maske: go in disguise

Oaten reeds: the pastoral pipe

scryne: a place in which to keep jewels hid: also 'shrine'

***Tanaquill*:** wife to Tarquin, an early king of Rome, she was famous for her virtue, but here she is identified with Gloriana, the Faerie Queene, whom Arthur has sought throughout the world. Arthur is the Briton Prince mentioned here. The reader will see that Spenser is trying to link Roman and British history in his story

***Jove*:** in Roman mythology the highest god in the heavens, corresponding to the Greek Zeus

***Venus*:** goddess of love who, with her son, Cupid (the one referred to here) is a deity often described in the image-pictures (iconography) of Spenser

Heben bow: bow made of ebony, the blackness of which suggests evil. See Shakespeare, *Hamlet*, I. 5. 62: 'with juice of cursed hebona in a vial' Claudius poisoned Hamlet's father

***Mart*:**	Mars. The union of Venus and Cupid and Mars signifies joy and harmony
***Phoebus*:**	another name for Apollo, the sun-god, son of Zeus
Vouchsafe:	deign, grant. Spenser is asking his dear 'dread', the Queen, to listen to him awhile

Canto I

Note: The numbers in brackets indicate stanza numbers.

The Red Crosse Knight is on his mission of mercy with Una (meaning Truth, the One) whose parents the Dragon (Satan) has expelled from their lands. Una rides upon an ass and is followed by a dwarf, who carries her necessities. The Red Crosse Knight is wearing the armour Una brought to Faerie Land for her champion but he has to learn his 'new force' (3). This 'new force' is the new life in Christ the knight has taken up for his mission, and it goes back to the Bible, to St Paul: 'And have put on the new man which is renewed in knowledge after the image of him that created him' (see the Bible, Colossians 3:10). Throughout this entire book we are reminded of the word 'force' in this sense.

A shower comes on and they take cover in a wood, the trees of which are beautifully described, but it only 'seemes' a 'Faire harbour' (7). They lose their way and come upon a 'hollow cave', which Una says is *Errours den*. The Red Crosse Knight, full of boldness, looks in and sees the hideous monster, a serpent with a huge tail, with her thousand young feeding off her poisonous dugs. The Red Crosse Knight strikes her and they fight. She entangles him with her tail, but when Una urges him to 'add faith unto [his] force' (19), he chokes the serpent so that she spews up a mess of books, pamphlets, frogs and toads. Out of her womb pours a 'spawne' of small offspring. Appalled by the stink the Knight beheads the monster. The small serpents rush to engorge themselves on their mother's blood until they burst. After this encounter the Knight and his companions have no difficulty in finding their way out of the forest which before was a labyrinth to them.

On their way, they meet an old hermit, with what looks like a Bible at his belt, but he later turns out to be Archimago, a false magician, and, like Error, a manifestation of Satan. As night is coming on he invites them to his hermitage 'down in a dale', where the Knight is to succumb to temptation. Archimago entertains them and speaks often of the Pope, saying many 'Hail Marys'. While his guests sleep Archimago calls up two spirits: one he sends to the house of Morpheus, god of sleep, to bring back a lustful dream; the other he frames out of 'liquid ayre' into a likeness of Una. The dream is placed upon the

Knight's head to disturb his sleep until he wakes to find the likeness of Una beside him. She tells him that it was for love of him she left her parents' lands, which makes him take pity on her. Nothing further takes place and he falls into a troubled sleep again.

NOTES AND GLOSSARY:

Canto: literally 'song', but used by Spenser (who took the word from the Italian poets Dante Alighieri (1265-1321) and Ludovico Ariosto (1474-1533)) to denote a section of a poem
***Patron*:** defender
pricking: spurring his horse
giusts: jousts; martial and ceremonial knightly encounters
ydrad: dreaded
earne: yearn
puissance: strength
Dragon: a beast of legend, with a great tail, who breathes fire, and who is often associated with the force of evil. Here he is Satan, the Devil himself
wimpled: folded
lore: learning
feend: fiend; the Dragon, Satan
needments: necessities. A word coined by Spenser
sayling Pine: ships and their masts were made out of pine
vine-prop Elme: vines were often grown round elms
meed: reward
still: ever
Eugh: the yew
Platane: the plane-tree
weene: think
labyrinth: a maze, artfully designed so that people may lose their way in it
Eftsoones: forthwith
courser: courtly name for a horse
full of . . . disdaine: exciting disdain
boughtes: coils
entraile: coiling
bale: injury
trenchand: sharp
enhaunst: raised up
dint: stroke
Tho: then
sterne: tail

gall: the place where, according to the old physiology, anger is located in the body
grate: agitate itself
parbreake: vomit
***Nilus*:** the river Nile in Egypt
avale: abate
reed: see
sinke: womb or bowels
welke: wane
ill bestedd: in a bad way
quited: returned the salute
sits not: is not fitting
mell: mix himself up with
forwearied: very wearied
baite: rest and feed
***Aue-Mary*:** Hail Mary, the prayer
***Morpheus*:** the god of sleep and dreams
***Pluto's* griesly Dame:** Pluto is god of the Underworld and his 'griesly Dame' is his wife Proserpina
***Gorgon*:** one of the underworld deities, here identified with the devil
***Cocytus*:** the river of lamentation in Hades, the underworld
***Styx*:** the river of death in Hades
***Tethys*:** wife of Neptune, who is god of the sea
***Cynthia*:** the moon
loft: air
swowne: faint
***Hecate*:** a female deity of the underworld, often linked with Proserpina
sent: senses
carke: anxiety
borne without her dew: born into life without regard for normal custom
***Graces*:** the three handmaids of the goddess Venus
***Hymen iō Hymen*:** the graces' song in praise of marriage. Hymen is the god of marriage
***Flora*:** the goddess of flowers, but also a harlot
ruth: pity
amate: dismay, but here also a pun on the word 'mate'
frayes: frightens
shend: reproach
beguiled of her art: disappointed in her

Canto II

Archimago transforms the spirit whom he had earlier sent to Morpheus for the lewd dream, into the semblance of a young squire, and makes him lie with the false Una, in 'vaine delight' (3). He then wakes the Red Crosse Knight and brings him to a place where he can spy upon their love-making. This throws the Knight into a fit of jealousy and despair, and he flees with the dwarf, after being prevented from slaying the couple in anger.

Una wakes up, and, finding her companions gone, sets off after them, but cannot catch them and wanders aimlessly. Archimago exults, but, hating Una intensely, takes upon himself the likeness of the Knight, so that he seems like St George, which is the figure which the Red Crosse Knight is to become *after* he slays the old Dragon.

The Knight encounters a Saracen, a non-Christian, pagan knight, Sans Foy (without Faith), who accompanies a very richly dressed lady, who, it turns out, is Duessa, or the Whore of Babylon, or Popery, or Mary Tudor. Sans Foy and the Knight engage in combat. Sans Foy is defeated, (after some delay, but the Red Crosse Knight is saved by his Shield of Faith), and the lady begs for mercy.

Her story is that she is the only daughter of a Great Emperor (the Church of Rome), who betrothed her to a faithful prince (Christ), who fell into the hands of his enemies and was killed. She says her name is Fidessa, and the Red Crosse Knight, taking pity on her, offers his protection.

The day being hot they take cover under two trees and he, wishing to deck her with a garland, pulls a branch from one of them. Blood seeps from the wound and the tree speaks. Fradubio tells his story: he and his lady Fraelissa once came upon a knight and another lady, very like Fraelissa. The other knight claimed that his lady was more beautiful and Fradubio fought and defeated him, taking his lady as 'prise martiall'. She turns out to have been none other than Duessa, who, by use of magic, persuaded Fradubio that his lady was vile. They left her in the waste, where she turned into a tree. Then one day Fradubio saw Duessa as she really was, while bathing (witches were supposed to have to assume their true shapes at certain times), and sought an opportunity to steal away, but Duessa, knowing how he felt, put a spell upon him, and took him to where Fraelissa, now a tree, stood, and planted him there. They are to stay metamorphosed in this way until they are bathed in a 'living well' (the water of life—see Canto XI). Duessa, who is present all the time, listening to the story, pretends to faint, and the Red Crosse Knight solicitously takes her in his arms and kisses her.

NOTES AND GLOSSARY:

Northerne wagoner: the constellation of the Plough
Chaunticlere: the cock
lusty-hed: lust
feigned: pretended
wex: grow
ment: joined together
***Hesperus*:** morning and evening star, Venus
***Tithones*:** Tithonus was the mortal lover of the dawn, Aurora, who was given immortality but not eternal youth
***Titan*:** another name for Phoebus, the god of the sun
stowre: time of distress
drift: plan
***Proteus*:** a sea-god, known for his ability to change his shape at will
Sarazin: Saracen, a pagan
Purfled: embroidered
owches: jewels
palfrey: courtly name for a horse
couch: settle (a spear) into the correct position for attack
rebut: recoil
quyteth: repays
scowre: run
lowre: frowne
***Tiberis*:** the river Tiber which flows through Rome
fone: foes
assaid: assailed
hind: deer
dainty they say maketh derth: coyness, they say, makes precious or dear
Astond: astounded
houe: rise
***Limbo*:** a part of Hell set aside for the unbaptised, a fitting place for Fradubio, who must be bathed in the 'living well' before he can be saved. The Knight too is in a kind of Limbo, as he too needs to be baptised, as is later revealed (Canto XI)
***Boreas*:** the north wind
cheualree: chivalry, a knightly system of the feudal period, with a code of honour that included religious, social and moral elements
dye: chance
treen mould: the form or mould of a tree

unweeting: unknowing
wist: knew
neather: lower
pight: planted

Canto III

The story returns to Una, and Spenser tells us how much he pities her in her wretchedness. One day she lies down to rest in the shade and a lion comes out of the forest, who first goes to attack her, but, smitten by her beauty, he licks her hands. The lion is Henry VIII, and he becomes her companion and champion. They meet a young girl, who, terrified at the sight of the lion and of the stranger runs to her mother's hovel. Una and her lion seek shelter there, but find it barred against them. The lion, however, smashes down the door. The old woman is a Papist and superstitious. Abessa is the daughter's name; that of the mother is Corceca. Reluctantly they give Una and the lion shelter for the night.

When it is dark there is a furious knocking. It is Kirkrapine, who specialises in thieving from churches, and he brings his booty to the two women, the younger of whom he uses as his whore. He breaks the door in but the lion savages him. Next morning Una and the lion leave, followed by Abessa and Corceca, who curse them. Archimago happens to pass, and gets news from them of Una, whom he is seeking in order to do her more harm. Soon he finds her and she, thinking he is the Red Crosse Knight, welcomes him back with great affection. Sans Loy (without Law) comes along, and, seeing the red cross on Archimago's shield, attacks, in revenge for his brother, Sans Foy. Archimago is unhorsed and Una appeals, in vain, to Sans Loy, to show him mercy as he lies on the ground. But when Sans Loy removes his opponent's helmet he sees that it is Archimago, the magician, and lets him go, as a 'friend' (39). Sans Loy then, inflamed with lust, lays hold of Una. The lion, rampant in heraldic posture, tries to smash the pagan's shield with his claws. But the pagan overcomes the lion and kills him. Una is now at the mercy of Sans Loy; she is his 'spoile' (43).

NOTES AND GLOSSARY:
fealtie: loyalty
deriu'd: diverted
none: no-one
ramping: rampant (a heraldic posture); standing on its hind legs, its forepaws raised in the air
***Aldeboran*:** a bright reddish star in the constellation of Taurus
***Cassiopeia's* chaire:** a constellation

that long wandering *Greek*: Ulysses, who, wishing to return to Ithaca and to his wife Penelope (after the siege of Troy), refused the love of the goddess Calypso and the immortality she offered

traynes: guile

derth: famine

fierce *Orion's* hound: Sirius, the dog star, whose rising marks the hottest days of the year

***Nereus*:** the oldest of the children of Tethys, who is the wife of Neptune

chauffed: chafed

***Lethe*:** one of the lakes in hell, the lake of forgetfulness

weene: intend

launcht: pierced

Canto IV

The Red Crosse Knight and Duessa (calling herself Fidessa) travel to the house of Pride, an elaborate building covered over with 'golden foile' (4), but built on sand, which 'flits' (5). The whole edifice is surmounted by a sun dial,* emphasising the worldliness of the place. The doorkeeper lets them into the presence of Pride, Lucifera, who tries to outshine the sun. Lucifera climbs into her chariot and begins a ceremonial progress of the seven deadly sins. The chariot is drawn by six different animals on which ride six of the sins (her 'sage counsellors'), she herself being the seventh.

The first, riding upon an ass, is Idlenesse, and beside him, on a swine, Gluttony, who is so fat and hot he wears only vine leaves. Lechery, the third sin of the flesh, rides upon a goat, bearing all the signs of the 'fowle evill' (26) of venereal disease. Coupled with him is the first of the three worldly sins, Avarice, who, riding upon a camel laden with gold, lives his life for himself alone. Next comes Enuie, riding upon a ravenous wolf, hating Avarice's gold and the pride of Lucifera, converting everything from good to bad by his spite. Beside him rides Wrath, upon a lion, nearly out of control in his rage, often repenting the damage done in his anger. Upon the wagon beam itself sits Satan goading them on with his whip, as they trample over dead men's skulls. They proceed out into the fields to take the air, and show off, Duessa getting as close as possible to Lucifera in the train.

Coming back they meet Sans Joy (without Joy), who, seeing that the Red Crosse Knight carries Sans Foy's shield as a trophy, attacks him. They are stopped by Lucifera, who commands them to fight in the

*A stone clock on which the time is told by the shadow of the sun as it moves across the sky. It was often used as a symbol for time and for the world.

lists (a chivalric jousting battle) the next day. That night they feast. When all are asleep Duessa steals to Sans Joy's room where she declares that she still loves his brother Sans Foy, but that she will devote herself to him if he defeats the Red Crosse Knight. She warns the pagan of the Knight's charmed shield and armour.

NOTES AND GLOSSARY:

lazars: lepers
farre over: high above
***Maluenu*:** ill-welcome
***Phoebus* fairest childe:** Phaeton, son of the sun-god, who took his father's chariot one day, but could not control the team of horses. He had to be killed by Jove for his irresponsible act
unequall: of different sizes
amis: monk's hood
Portesse: a priestly missal or breviary carried by Roman Catholic priests
esloyne: withdraw
chalenged essoyne: claimed exemption
whally: staring
chaw: mouth
maw: guts
griple: grasping
choler: the humour that causes anger
woxen wood: grown mad
scath: harm
Splene: temper
Palsey: a spastic disease traditionally associated with anger
Saint *Francis* fire: erysipelas, a disease that leads to livid inflammation of the skin
darrayne: engage in order to justify a claim
recreant: cowardly
renuerst: turned upside down
can: did
faytor: impostor
For that: because

Canto V

The next day the Red Crosse Knight and Sans Joy take their places in the field of tilt (the place set aside for ceremonial jousting, sometimes called the tilt yard) where they fight fiercely, the one for right, the other for wrong. The Knight is nearly overcome, but hearing Duessa's voice he is inspired with new courage and subdues his opponent, who is carried off on a 'darksome clowd' (13), brought down by Duessa. The Red Crosse Knight's wounds are treated and Duessa weeps, like the crocodile (18).

Darkness coming on, Duessa goes to Night, whom she finds coming out of her den with her 'coleblacke steedes' (20). She appeals to Night, questioning her as to why she allows her nephews, the Saracens, to be defeated by the Red Crosse Knight. Night replies that it is 'destinee' (25) (a suitably pagan reply), but that the Knight will pay in his blood for what he has spilled (reminding us of the old law: an eye for an eye, a tooth for a tooth). Together they fly in Night's chariot to where Sans Joy lies in blood, during which time the dogs bark and the owls shriek, knowing something unnatural is afoot. They take him down into Hades where all the classical scenes out of Virgil's *Aeneid*, Book VI, are described: they meet the terrible Cerberus, the many-headed dog of hell, who lolls forth a 'bloodie flaming tong'; they see Ixion being turned on a wheel; and Tityus, whose liver is being devoured by a vulture. They come, eventually, to the object of Night's quest, Aesculapius, the healer, whose story is told—he is in Hades because he restored Hippolytus, a mortal, to life. Now Night begs him to do the same for Sans Joy, whom they leave there.

When Duessa returns to Pride's palace, she finds the Red Crosse Knight gone. The 'wary' dwarf had told him that in the dungeons of the castle he had found great numbers of 'captive wretched thrals' (45), victims of pride. They are named: among them are Nebuchadnezzar, Croesus, Semiramis, and Cleopatra. The Red Crosse Knight made his escape by the back door, and had to pick his way through great heaps of corpses. His last view is 'a dunghill of dead carkases', the 'dreadfull spectacle of that sad house of *Pride*' (53).

NOTES AND GLOSSARY:

doughtie:	valiant
***Ynd*:**	India
blesse:	brandish
rauine:	spoil
souce:	strike
german:	kinsman
can:	did
mew:	den
***Daemogorgon*:**	chaos
***Aveugle*:**	(*French*) blind, a folk name for a blind old man
excheat:	spoil, gain
unlich:	unlike
cruddy:	clotted
***Auernus*:**	Avernus, a lake that leads into Hades or hell

***Furies*:** the hellish spirits of discord
brast: burst
biliue: quickly
***Acheron*:** one of the rivers of Hades
***Phlegeton*:** another of the rivers of Hades
***Cerberus*:** the dog guarding the entrance to Hades
lilled: lolled
felly gnarre: fiercely snarl
***Ixion*:** one of the tormented in Hades, who is tied to a wheel
***Sisyphus*:** one of the tormented in Hades, who has to push a stone up a hill, which always rolls down again once he gets to the top
***Tantalus*:** another of the damned, who suffers from thirst, but whose lips never can touch the water of the river
***Tityus*:** another of the damned, whose liver is continually eaten by a vulture
***Typhoeus*:** one of the damned, who is stretched on a rack
***Theseus*:** another of the damned, who is condemned to sit in a chair of forgetfulness
***Aesculapius*:** god of healing and son of Apollo
***Hippolytus*:** his story is told in the text
recure: refresh
noyous: obnoxious
albe: although
provd king of *Babylon*: Nebuchadnezzar, who set up an idol to be worshipped, until through God's decree he was deposed and treated like a beast of the field. See the Bible, Daniel 3-6
***Croesus*:** a king of Lydia, famous for his riches
***Antiochus*:** a king of Syria who defiled the temple in Jerusalem. See the Bible, Apocrypha, I Machabees 1
***Nimrod*:** the first tyrant after the Flood and founder of Babylon
***Ninus*:** the first to make war and founder of Nineveh
that mighty Monarch: Alexander the Great (356-323BC)
***Ammon's* sonne:** Alexander the Great claimed that he was born as a serpent and that his father was Jupiter Ammon (another name for the Roman god Jove)
***Romulus*:** the first king of Rome
***Tarquin*:** the last king of Rome
***Lentulus*:** a Roman patrician, who attempted to burn the city

***Scipio*:** a famous Roman general (237-183BC), who subdued Hannibal in North Africa in 202BC at the battle of Zama

***Hanniball*:** a general from Carthage who fought against Rome. He crossed the Alps into Italy and defeated the Romans at Lake Trasimene (217BC). He was defeated by Scipio in 202BC

***Sylla*:** more properly Sulla, Lucius Cornelius (138-78BC), a Roman general and statesman. He served under Marius in Africa and Gaul. Of patrician lineage, he fell out with Marius and expelled him from Rome. He became dictator and ruled tyranically, ending his life in dissipation

***Marius*:** a Roman general (157-86BC), who served in Africa and in Gaul. Of humble origins, he was jealous of Sulla (Sylla), and war broke out between them

***Caesar*:** Caius Julius Caesar (100 or 102BC-44BC), leader of the democratic party, who formed the first triumvirate with Pompey and Crassus in 60BC. He spent nine years subduing Gaul, including Britain. Pompey went over to the aristocrats and the Senate called on Caesar to resign his command. In reply Caesar took over all Italy. He was made Emperor, and his person declared divine, but he was assassinated on 15 March 44BC

***Pompey*:** Gnaeus Pompeius Magnus (106-48BC) supported Sulla in the war with Marius, was made consul, and entered Rome in triumph three times after his conquests. At first he and Caesar were allies, but then they fell out. In the end he fled to Egypt, where he was murdered

***Antonius*:** Mark Antony, a Roman soldier and statesman (*c.*83BC-30BC), he was related to Julius Caesar. After Caesar's assassination he and Octavian, Caesar's heir, and Lepidus, ruled together over the whole Roman world. He defeated Brutus and Cassius in Macedonia, then went to Egypt, where he fell in love with Cleopatra. Octavian and Antony quarrelled and at the Battle of Actium (31BC) Antony was defeated by the Roman fleet. He returned to Egypt and killed himself by throwing himself on his sword

***Semiramis*:** wife to Ninus, founder of Nineveh, who tried to commit incest with her son

***Sthenoboea*:** she lusted after her brother-in-law, Bellerophon. When he married she killed herself

***Cleopatra*:** Queen of Egypt (69-30BC) and mistress of Julius Caesar and Antonius. Antonius became infatuated with her and lived with her in luxury in Alexandria, neglecting his duties in Rome. After his defeat she killed herself by, it is said, putting an asp (a venomous snake) to her breast

Posterne: back door

Lay-stall: a place where the dead are laid; or a dung-heap

Canto VI

We return to Una, whom we left at the end of Canto III at the mercy of the pagan, Sans Loy. He takes her into the 'forrest wilde' (3)—always in Spenser associated with error and danger—and at first tries to win her over by blandishments, but failing in this he resorts to force. She cries out in distress, and a group of fauns and satyrs (fauns are benign wood creatures, thought to be woodland deities; satyrs are more lascivious, being half men, half goats) hearing her screams, come to her assistance. Sans Loy rides off.

At first Una is terrified of the wood creatures, but they show themselves most obedient and courteous to her, kneeling down and kissing her feet, and worshipping her as a queen. They dance to her, crown her with an olive garland, then bring her to their lord, old Sylvanus, who thinks of his 'ancient love' (17), Cyparissus, a youth to whom he was much attached, but who turned into the cypress tree when Sylvanus slew his pet deer by mischance. (This story comes from the Latin poet Ovid (43BC-AD17).) Una stays with the wood creatures a long time, and they treat her as a goddess, despite the fact that she tries to restrain them. This is their 'barbarous truth' (12).

One day a knight called Sir Satyrane comes into the forest. He is the off-spring of Thyamis (passion), a lady neglected by her husband Therion (wild beast), and a satyr, whom Thyamis met in the forest when, distracted with passion, she was seeking her husband. Sir Satyrane was raised among the animals, and is fierce and courageous. He helps Una to get away from the satyrs and out of the 'forrest wilde'.

When they get to the plain the first person they see is a pilgrim, who turns out to be Archimago, yet again. To Una's enquiries about the Red Crosse Knight he replies, falsely, that he saw him killed that very day by none other than Sans Loy, who in Canto III had defeated what *seemed* to be the Red Crosse Knight, but was in fact Archimago himself in disguise. Archimago here is recounting his own defeat at the hands of Sans Loy, who did not kill him, and concluding it tragically to throw Una into despair. Una and the Red Crosse Knight are still lost in a confusion of treachery and guile.

Sir Satyrane goes off to find Sans Loy (who had earlier tried to rape Una) and he comes upon him by a fountain. Sans Loy makes it clear to Sir Satyrane that he had not killed the Red Crosse Knight, but that Archimago had been wearing armour very like that of Una's champion. Satyrane and Sans Loy set to; Una comes along and the sight of her inflames the pagan, and he makes after her again. This increases the force of Satyrane's attack. Una, frightened by Sans Loy's approach, flees, followed by Archimago. The fight is still undecided when the Canto closes.

NOTES AND GLOSSARY:

foole-happie:	fortunate
dreed:	object of awe
t'efforce:	to overcome by force
bet:	beaten
implyes:	conceals
blubbred:	wet with tears
faine:	glad
stadle:	a tree trunk used as a support
***Bacchus*:**	the Greek god of wine and revelry
***Cybele*:**	a Phrygian goddess of the powers of nature who was honoured in wild rites
***Dryope*:**	the consort of Faunus, a spirit of the forest
***Pholoe*:**	a nymph beloved of Pan, god of pastures and woods
***Hamadryades*:**	wood-nymphs
***Naiades*:**	freshwater nymphs
***Labryde*:**	the name means turbulent, greedy
venery:	wild animals (a pun on 'lust')
noursled:	nursed
Pardale:	female leopard
raught:	reached
***Jacob's staff*:**	a pilgrim's staff
thrild:	pierced
raile:	pour

Canto VII

We return to Duessa, who, finding that the Red Crosse Knight has left the house of Pride, goes out to seek him and finds him by a fountain-side, feeding upon the 'cooling shade'. Together they enjoy the pleasantness of the place, but the Red Crosse Knight is unaware of its true nature: the water he drinks is enfeebling, having been cursed by Diana. His 'manly forces' fail, and when the giant Orgoglio comes, the Red Crosse Knight is unready, having taken his armour off, and unable to defend himself.

Orgoglio, meaning Pride, is the son of the earth and the wind, and carries with him a great club of oak, with which he attacks the Red Crosse Knight. His huge stroke misses, but the rush of wind knocks the Knight senseless. Orgoglio is about to kill him when Duessa appeals to him to spare the Knight, offering herself as his reward. Orgoglio decks her out as the whore of Babylon, and she wears the Papal 'triple crowne' (16). Orgoglio sits her upon a monstrous beast with seven heads, the beast of Revelation 17:3: 'I saw a woman sitting upon a scarlet coloured beast, full of names of blasphemy, having seven heads and ten horns.' Orgoglio then throws the Red Crosse Knight into a dungeon.

The dwarf, left alone, picks up his master's armour, and very soon meets Una, in flight from the renewed attentions of Sans Loy, in the middle of his fight with Satyrane. When she sees the dwarf with the armour she faints. The dwarf revives her but when she returns to consciousness she cries out in despair that 'earthly sight can nought but sorrow breed' (23). The dwarf tells her of her Knight's misadventures and she sets out to find out if he is alive or dead.

And then she meets a Knight whose armour shines in the distance like the sun. He is none other than Prince Arthur himself, chancing to come along at the most critical moment. His armour is described in detail: his helmet, shaped like a dragon; his shield hewn out of one piece of diamond which has the property of affrighting the heavens themselves; and his spear of ebony which links him with Cupid and so with love.

Arthur attempts to make Una tell her story, but at first she feels she cannot convey the depth of her sorrow. He argues with her, pointing out how reason can 'repaire' (41) the weaknesses of the flesh that lead the spirit into despair, and this '[settles] in her gratious thought' (42). She then tells him of her parents: how they held sway in Eden (we know she is referring to Eden because she names the rivers associated with Paradise in Genesis); and how the Dragon destroyed their kingdom. They now live barred up in a brazen castle to which the Dragon lays siege. Many knights have tried to free them, but all have failed, the Dragon growing stronger with each foiled attempt. She then tells of the Red Crosse Knight, how she found him at Faerie Court, how she lost him through the guile of Archimago, and how he now lies a prisoner in Orgoglio's dungeon. Arthur promises her he will not forsake her until he has freed her captive knight, and they proceed guided by the dwarf.

NOTES AND GLOSSARY:

bayes: bathes

***Diane*:** goddess of the hunt and chastity

***Phoebe*:** another name for Diana

graile: gravel

***Aeolus*:** the wind

mace: a club-like weapon, usually spiked

darrayne: fight

pouldred: powdered

yron Engin: the cannon

Leman: lover

***Alcides*:** Hercules, who overcame the Hydra, a beast whose many heads grew again as soon as they were cut off

***Stremona*:** a river in Thrace

***Lerna*:** a lake where the Hydra was said to have grown

poynant: piercing

seeled: closed

stound: time

assay: trial

bauldrich: the belt worn from the right shoulder across the breast to support the sword and its scabbard

tong: pin

horrid: bristling (the Latin sense of the word)

beuer: visor

***Selinis*:** the town where the palm, given to victors, grew

Adamant: a rock as hard as diamond

***Merlin*:** a legendary Welsh magician, who aided Arthur and the Knights of the Round Table of Arthurian legend

canon bit: a smooth round bit

rowels: knobs for the chain

staid: constant

paire: impair

***Phison, Euphrates and Gehon*:** three rivers of Paradise as described in Genesis. The fourth river mentioned in Genesis, the Tigris, is included in the Euphrates

***Tartary*:** the lowest part of the infernal regions in Hades, where the giants who rebelled against the gods were put

***Cleopolis*:** the city of Glory, London in its mythological aspect, related to the later Jerusalem of William Blake (1757-1827)

disauenturous: unfortunate

mall: mace

Canto VIII

This canto shows us how Arthur, or 'heavenly grace', 'upholds' the Red Crosse Knight (1); and Una, in 'steadfast truth [acquits] him out of all' (1): that is, she absolves him from all blame for having fallen into Orgoglio's captivity. The reader should study every word in the first stanza with great care. The Red Crosse Knight is to be delivered from evil by the intervention of grace (Prince Arthur), who is guided by Una (single and steadfast truth).

Arthur, led by the dwarf, goes to Orgoglio's castle, and summons the giant to battle on a small bugle, the sound of which is as thrilling as the sound of the trumpet of Revelation itself, at which it hints. The giant comes out of his bower, where he has been dallying with Duessa, who comes out with him, riding upon her beast. The giant and Arthur fight. Orgoglio's first blow misses; he drives his huge club into the ground; Arthur slices off his arm which falls like a block; blood gushes from the trunk, like water from the rock that Moses struck. Duessa comes on her beast to assist him, but Arthur's squire stands in the way. Through her magic cup, which she carries, Duessa weakens him. He collapses, and the beast fastens his claws on him. Arthur comes to his squire's assistance, slices off one of the beast's seven heads, thereby filling the field with the filthy gore that pours from the monster's wound. The giant strikes Arthur with his club, using his remaining left hand and knocks him to the ground, but when this happens Arthur's terrible shield is uncovered. Its supernatural light, associated with the second coming of Christ, blinds the monster. Arthur cuts off the giant's leg at the knee, and he tumbles down. Then Arthur beheads him, at which he deflates, like an 'emptie bladder' (24). Duessa tries to escape but the squire holds her back. Una thanks Arthur and the squire. Hearing the Red Crosse Knight calling for help, Arthur goes into Orgoglio's castle.

There he finds an old man Ignaro (Ignorance), who is Orgoglio's father, but to all Arthur's questions he can find no answers. Arthur takes the keys of all the doors from Ignaro, and makes his way to a splendid chamber, the floor of which is covered with the blood of innocents, martyrs for the true faith. From an altar there comes the sound of their voices, crying out to God for vengeance. At last he comes to the Red Crosse Knight's cell, and hears him crying out of the depths of his despair, that he is 'in balefull darkness bound' (38). Arthur smashes down the door. There is a filthy smell, and when he enters, there is no floor but a 'deepe descent'. This is the depth of despair.

Arthur raises the Knight up and brings him out to the light, but he is withered and exhausted. Una greets him now in sickness ('woe') and in health ('wele') (43). The Red Crosse Knight is given the choice as to what to do about Duessa, but Una is against killing her. They strip her of her borrowed robes and her falsehood stands revealed in all its horror and filth. Naked, she is seen to have a fox's tail, 'with dong all fowly dight' (48). She is like the whore of Babylon in the Bible, Revelation 17:16: 'And the ten horns which thou sawest upon the beast, these shall hate the whore, and shall make her desolate and naked'. She then goes into the wilderness away from the sight of men.

NOTES AND GLOSSARY:

snubbes: root snags
food: feud
Cymbrian plaine: Denmark, named after the tribe that inhabited it
kindly rage: natural lust
quayed: quailed, daunted
seize: fasten
carefull: full of care
dites: lifts
slight: trick
vsuree: interest
better dayes: the better part of his life
pourtrahed: portrayed
empeach: hinder
enlargen: set free
nicer: too fastidious
bits: food (that is, bites)
bowrs: muscles
scald: scall, a disease of the scalp, in which it is covered with scabs
talaunts: talons
counterfesaunce: deceit
dainty: precious

Canto IX

Arthur cannot tell his lineage, because it is still hidden from him. When he was a child he was taken from his parents (who were royal) by Merlin and given to Timon (meaning honour) to be fostered. In response to Una's inquiry he tells both the Knight and her that he has come to Faery Land driven by a 'forced fury' (7) in his breast, which he attributes to God's will. He recounts how, as a youth, he would mock those who were in love until one day, full of energy and 'jollitie', tired out with 'raunging the forest wide' (12), he lay down on the grass and fell asleep. A 'royal Mayd' came to him in a dream, who, on parting from him, told him she was the Faerie Queene. His vow is that he will not rest until he finds her (which, we know from the letter to Raleigh, he was to have done in Book XII).

Before they part, Arthur and the Red Crosse Knight exchange gifts: Arthur gives the Knight a diamond box containing a 'liquor pure' (Christ's blood) and the Red Crosse Knight gives Arthur the New Testament.

The Knight is still weak from his incarceration in Orgoglio's castle. The next person they met is Sir Trevisan, who is fleeing in terror from Despair. The Knight asks him to take him to Despair's cabin so he can test himself against him. Despair's cabin is set in a wild melancholy place, under a craggy cliff, which is like a grave (33) in that it craves more corpses. They find Despair himself musing sadly, sitting on the ground, his hair unkempt, his dress disordered and uncared for, looking like a traditional figure of melancholy. At his feet lies Trevisan's friend, Sir Terwin (whom Despair has persuaded to commit suicide), dead in his own life-blood. The Red Crosse Knight accuses Despair of being guilty of the death of Terwin, and says that he must pay for it with his own blood (which the reader will recognise as the theology of the old law, not the new, of which love must be the guiding principle) (37). Despair then speaks of the weariness of life, its error and pointlessness, how all is determined by luck (41-7). The identity of the speaker of these lines is not clear; it could be the Knight himself speaking, which would be appropriate, because he is overcome by Despair, so that in a sense he is now that figure in the cabin under the forlorn cliff. In a picture Despair shows him the damned ghosts in Hell.

He then brings various instruments of death and at last a knife, but Una snatches it from the Red Crosse Knight and arouses his faith by reminding him of God's justice and mercy, that he is 'chosen' (53).

NOTES AND GLOSSARY:

thewes: ways
he me brought: 'he' refers to Merlin
byliue: forthwith
***Rauran*:** a hill in North Wales. Arthur's upbringing is located in Wales in order to link him with the Tudors (Henry VIII and Elizabeth I), who had Welsh origins
nouriture: upbringing
respire: take breath
kindly: natural
prickt forth: decked out
embayd: bathed
tyne: trouble, pain
onely worthy you: you alone (are) worthy

incontinent:	straightaway
Eft:	again
nathemore:	not at all
whyleare:	a while before
repriefe:	insult
knees:	cliffs
price:	pay for
uneath:	in unease
Centonell:	sentinel
roome:	station
droome:	drum
Miscreant:	misbeliever
dant:	daunt
ouercrow:	triumph over
well of life:	the heart
hand-writing:	see the Bible, St Paul's Epistle to the Colossians 2:14: 'And putting out the hand-writing of ordinances that was against us, which was contrarie to us, he even toke it out of the way, and fastened it upon the crosse.' (Quoted here from the Geneva Bible, a Bible produced and published in Geneva in 1560 by English Protestant Puritans, who had taken refuge there during the reign of the Catholic Queen Mary)
carle:	churl
unbid:	not prayed for

Canto X

Una, seeing that the Red Crosse Knight is exhausted ('weake and raw') (2), and therefore liable to succumb to temptation, resolves to bring him to the house of Holinesse, that he may be strengthened for the coming ordeal, in which he will have to face the Dragon. Dame Caelia (meaning 'heavenly') is the matron of the house, and she lives there with her three daughters: Fidelia (faith), Speranza (hope) and Charissa (charity). The door through which they gain entrance is tended by Humility and is 'streight and narrow' (quoting the Bible, Matthew 7:14, 'strait is the gate, and narrow is the way, which leadeth unto life'). The Knight and Una meet Dame Caelia and Fidelia and Speranza (Charissa, being love, has just given birth to a child, and so cannot be seen.) The two daughters approach in a ceremony which is, in its simplicity and faith, meant to comment on the brash show of Lucifera's pageant of the Seven Deadly Sins in Canto IV.

Fidelia instructs the Red Crosse Knight in the Book of Life and shows him how to read its mysteries, revealing to him also the miracles of which faith is capable. Glimpsing perfection, he is inclined again to succumb to Despair, but Speranza gives him her anchor of hope to which he may cling. His plight is still desperate, and, Dame Caelia, fully familiar with the torments of aggrieved conscience, sends for Patience. But the inward corruption remains. He fasts, and Amendment comes, to pluck out the rotting infection in him; Penance disciplines him; Remorse nips his heart; and Repentance washes all the blots of sin away. He is brought to Charissa, now recovered from her delivery, and taught the commandment of love and good works. Mercy brings him to a Hostel ('Hospitall') in which are seen the corporal works associated with her. In the stanza devoted to that mercy which has charge of the burial of the dead, Spenser speaks in his own voice, to pray that in death his body be not desecrated: 'Ah dearest God me graunt, I dead be not defould' (42). Having been taught by Mercy, the Red Crosse Knight is brought to Contemplation, an old man in a house by a chapel on top of a hill. Contemplation brings the Knight to the top of a mountain and shows him the holy city, the new Jerusalem of Revelation. The angels ascend and descend to and from Heaven and go into the city, where all the Saints are. It far surpasses Cleopolis (London), though Contemplation says that Cleopolis is the fairest of all cities on earth, and that in serving Una he is serving the 'soveraigne Dame' (59), none other than Elizabeth I herself.

He is told that when he comes, at last, to the new Jerusalem, he will be Saint George, appropriate for a 'man of earth' (52), for George means 'ploughman'. The Red Crosse Knight is puzzled that Contemplation says he is of English blood: he thought that he was from Faerie land but it is explained that he is a changeling, stolen by a faerie from England before his baptism, and discovered in Faerie land by a ploughman; hence his name, and his lowly appearance at the Faerie court. In stanza 67 he is blinded by the revelation granted to him through Contemplation. Knowing who he is, he now dedicates himself to his task, accepting God's will. His forces are gathered together again. He has begun to find himself: 'At last when as himself he gan to find'(68).

NOTES AND GLOSSARY:

recouered: got over
bidding of her bedes: saying her prayers
thewes: manners
fere: husband
pledges: here children, in that children are pledges of their love
franklin: freeholder

euer-dying dread: constant fear of death
***Fidelia*:** Faith
***Speranza*:** Hope
***Charissa*:** Charity
agraste: favoured with grace
streight: strict
disple: discipline
vneath: difficult
Hospitall: hostel
why: for which
stowre: assault
throw: throe
engraue: bury
wonne: persuaded
fordonne: exhausted (compare the slang expression, 'done for')
sead: seed
assoiled: absolved
yod: went
sam: together
nominate: call
reft: took
find: recover

Canto XI

Una and the Knight head for Una's 'native soyle' (2). She can see, from a distance, her parents looking out from their brazen keep, where the Dragon, Satan, has them under siege. At the sight of the Red Crosse Knight's shining armour the huge Dragon half flies, half runs towards them. He is described in all his horror: the brazen plates covering his entire body, like Leviathan in the Bible, in the Book of Job; the two steel-sharp stings in his tail; the triple row of iron teeth; and the appalling stench of sulphur and smoke from his gorge. After some initial exchanges the Dragon flies into the air and picks up the Knight and his horse. Struggling, the Knight forces the Dragon to release him, and he wounds the beast under the wing. Enraged, the Dragon blasts the Knight with a 'flake of fire' (26) which boils him in his armour, and, when he is thus weakened, the Dragon fells him with a blow of his tail. Behind the Knight's back is the well of life, into which he falls, an indication that he will rise again the next day. It is now night-time. This is the Knight's baptism as well, and he rises 'new-borne' (34) on the next day, his hands 'baptized' (36). He wounds the Dragon deeply in the skull.

The Dragon stings him with his tail, piercing through the shield of faith, but the Knight hacks off five joints of the tail (indicating the five senses), at which the Dragon retaliates by jumping on the shield itself, and grasping it in its talons. The Knight, smashing at them with his sword, gets one free, then cuts the other off completely, though it still retains its grip on the shield. A blast of fire knocks him back and he falls in the mire, but beside him grows the tree of life itself, from which flows a stream of balm which saves him from death. Near it grows the tree of knowledge from which Adam and Eve ate. The tree of life is also the Cross which has saved mankind, and Holy Communion. The second night comes on and the Knight sleeps, 'besmeared' (50) with the balm of life.

On the third day he rises again and slays the Dragon, who rushes at him with his jaws open wide, by thrusting deep into the monster's mouth with his sword.

NOTES AND GLOSSARY:

vneath: underneath
vntill: towards
yede aloof: go aside
equipage: equipment
blaze: proclaim
pennes: the ribs of the wings
boughts: coils
stouping: descending
hagard hauke: untamed hawk
hable: able
pounces: anterior claws
trusse: seize and carry off
disseized of his gryping grosse: deprived of his gripping strength
thrillant: piercing
can: did
trenchand: sharp
buffe: blow
beguyled: foiled
swinged: singed
Champion: Hercules, when he put on the garment soaked in the blood of Nessus the centaur, half-man, half-horse
respire: live
hot: was called
***Silo*:** Siloam, the pool in the Gospel of St John where the man born blind was healed by washing. See the Bible, John 9:7

***Jordan*:**	the river in which Christ was baptised by St John the Baptist. See the Bible, Matthew 3:16
***Bath*:**	the English city the waters of which were renowned for their curative properties
***Spau*:**	a watering-place in Belgium, twenty miles south-west of Liège (like Bath in England)
***Cephise*:**	a river in Greece, famous for its healing waters
***Hebrus*:**	a river in Thrace, into which the head of Orpheus was thrown
iournall:	daily
Eyas:	young, untamed hawk
buxome:	unresisting
intended:	extended
seasd:	penetrated
diseasd:	tormented
wedge:	metal being worked in a forge
***Aetna*:**	Etna, famous volcano
stew:	cauldron
back retyred:	on being drawn back

Canto XII

A watchman on the wall of the brazen castle sees that the Dragon has been defeated and old Adam is overjoyed. All his people flock out to greet the visitor and to acclaim him. A little vignette describes how the ordinary folk fearfully approach the great beast: one mother snatches back a child who had started to play with the talons.

After a well-ordered and ceremonious feast the Knight tells the story of his adventures. Adam asks him to stay with them but the Red Crosse Knight reveals that he must return to serve the Faerie Queene for six years in her fight against the paynim (pagan) king, who here is Philip II of Spain as well as the world of creation itself, which Holinesse has to fight until the seventh day, when, the six days of creation at an end, he can rest from his Christian labours and be united with Una, Truth.

Adam promises his daughter to the Red Crosse Knight and she comes in, clad in a cloth of silver and silk. Her 'blazing brightnesse' (23) is described, and the vows of betrothal are about to be made when a messenger bursts in, none other than Archimago himself, bearing letters from Duessa, claiming that she and the Knight are promised to each other. The Knight seems to have left out the detail of his dalliance with Duessa in Canto VII (7) in the account he gave of his adventures (he is still not one with Una, Truth), but now he tells of the false Duessa who pretended to be Fidessa. Una speaks up for him as well, and recognises Archimago under his disguise. He is arrested and cast into the dungeon and the vows are made.

The Knight and Una declare their love for each other, and the betrothal and promise of marriage are celebrated by sprinkling the doorposts with wine, feasting, and perfuming the house. Music is played and the wonderful ninefold harmony of the music of the spheres sounds throughout the palace. The Knight takes great joy in his mistress, but he does not forget that he must return to Faerie Land. The canto and the book conclude with an image of the ship coming into harbour, the intended journey finished, for a time.

NOTES AND GLOSSARY:

Vere: Let out
beare up with: sail before the wind to
tort: wrong
habiliments: clothes
Timbrels: tambourines
enraung'd: varying
defeasance: defeat
purveyance: provisions
importune: grievous
emprize: enterprise
preace: press
In sort as: in the way that
intendiment: careful consideration
t'inuegle: to beguile
improvided: unforeseen
practicke: tricky
turne: task
housling: house
Teade: torch

Part 3

Commentary

Kind

'Kind' was a technical term in the Renaissance, and indeed for a long time after. It indicates the branch of poetry to which a given poem belongs. *The Faerie Queene* is an epic, as was Homer's *Odyssey*, or Virgil's *Aeneid*. Other kinds were: tragedy, elegy, pastoral.

The Faerie Queene, however, is more than just an epic; it is an allegorical romantic epic. The Renaissance (which means 'rebirth') was a period in which classical learning received a new impetus with the discovery of the Greek texts of Plato which had for a long time only been known through Latin translations. It was a period during which Western man made all kinds of technological, geographical, and psychological discoveries, a time when new avenues of consciousness opened up in every sphere of activity from the astonishing power and beauty of a sculpture by Michelangelo (1475-1564), to the mathematical complexity of the formulae Johannes Kepler (1571-1630) thought out to describe the apparent irregularities in the orbit of Mars. Michel de Montaigne (1533-92) pondered the life-systems and behaviour of humanity when he wrote of the cannibals discovered in the vast new territories of South America.

The Renaissance witnessed, then, not just a rebirth of classical learning, but a new phase of human development, such as, perhaps, we are witnessing now. The epic was the grandest and most impressive *kind* of verbal art in the old world, and one of the reasons why it was so was because it told the story of the individual emerging from the anonymity of the tribe or the clan and by so doing defining that tribe or clan. Ancient Greece is to some extent typified in the courage, endurance, and technical skill of Ulysses, the hero of the *Odyssey*; and, much more explicitly, Rome is typified in the adventures of Aeneas, in Virgil's *Aeneid*. Virgil's epic is a poem about the emergence of Rome from the ashes of Troy.

In the Renaissance, when a new phase of human awareness was taking place, it was natural that poets should turn to the epic, not just to emulate the ancients (though that undoubtedly was a stimulus), but also because they would respond to the sort of experience the epic *kind* always presented, that is, an experience of emergence, of definition.

For a new kind of man, there would be a new kind of epic, defining and representing all his new-found attributes—his new bravery, his increase in understanding, his deepened awareness, his rediscovered glory.

Homer and Virgil were Spenser's models, but he also had the more recent achievements of Italian epics to look towards and to rival. Ludovico Ariosto's (1474-1533) *Orlando Furioso* (1532) was a romantic epic ('romantic' in the sense that it relied on late medieval romance, in which the knight's struggle on behalf of the good, and his love for his lady, are closely intertwined). It will be clear that Spenser follows this model in his romantic epic: the Red Crosse Knight's task, the killing of the Dragon, is totally bound up with his love for Una (Truth) and he is, eventually, to be one with her.

Torquato Tasso's (1544-95) *Gerusalemme Liberata* (*Jerusalem Delivered*), published in 1581, was another influence. Here too we have the knight and his lady; magical allurements; and the holy city of Jerusalem itself, which is to figure so strongly in the vision accorded to the Red Crosse Knight in Canto X of Book I.

Spenser's Jerusalem, like Tasso's, is also the holy city of Chapter 21 of the biblical Book of Revelation, which reminds us that Spenser's epic combines classical, medieval, contemporary European and Christian elements. Spenser's hero, in Book I especially, is the new man, or at least he is the old man who is awakened into a new phase of life through the power of Truth, and thereby given the capacity to see what the new Jerusalem will be like, and the energy to defeat the old Dragon. Book I depicts the Christian hero, the *miles Christi* (soldier of Christ) gaining definition and strength. Spenser's poem is an epic of the Protestant Renaissance. Not only does it depict the awakening of a new and individual strength in the hero of Book I, it also seeks to bring about a revelation, a growth of understanding in the reader, through its method. That method is allegory.

Allegory

Allegory, Spenser tells us in the letter to Raleigh, is a 'darke conceit', which means a slightly obscure sustained relationship between different levels of meaning. Another way of putting this is to say that in an allegory we have a story, the parts of which, as the story proceeds, unfold another meaning, which is gradually apprehended in the course of the narration.

It is not surprising that allegory was a favourite method for writers who wanted to bring home to their readers the truths which they desired to present, because allegory not only engages the imaginative part of the mind, in calling up pictures, scenes, and so on; it also attributes to these scenes and pictures a meaning, which the reader, to some extent, discovers for himself. Allegory involves the reader in that the writer draws him to participate imaginatively in discovering the 'darke conceit' and in working out its meanings. Reading becomes a form of mental, moral and intellectual discipline. It was a method well-suited to the ideals of Protestant morality and ethic. A reader should not just let the meanings come to him, he should, to a certain extent, work them out for himself, because they are his approach to the truth.

Spenser tells a story of knights and ladies, of Arthur and England, and of the conquest of a dragon by a hero who looked unlikely to begin with. But, from the outline of the religious and political background to Spenser's poem, it will be clear to the student that Spenser's story is also presenting an attitude, uncovering a way of thinking about the events of recent history, especially the reign of the Tudor dynasty. This is, of course, not all that Spenser is conveying or hinting at in his allegory: his method is not monovalent, or one-to-one; that is, Una is not *just* Elizabeth. His method is polyvalent, in that a figure or an event can attach itself to a number of different meanings, and it is the cluster of meaning that gives the significance, and that challenges the reader to reflect and expand upon his own received thinking. Una is also the One; she is associated with the sun; she is Truth; she is the woman in Revelation 12 who flees from a dragon; she is the source of the growth of faith in the civilised soul; she is the Church of Christ on earth; and she is also, in some respects, Christ himself. This is how Spenser's mind works. He sometimes confuses the reader by the weight of significance he will attach to a single figure, but the basic concept is usually simple enough: here Una is One. His syncretism (the elaboration of meanings outlined above) is constructed on a sound and simple base.

The main historical elements of the allegory can be set down here, in bald outline, though the student should be warned that the meaning of each of the characters goes well beyond this specific identification.

Una:	Elizabeth
Red Crosse Knight:	the Church of England
Error:	the Catholic Church
Archimago:	the Pope
Duessa:	Mary Tudor, and, to some extent, Mary Queen of Scots
Lion:	Henry VIII
Corceca:	superstitious Catholicism
Sans Foy: Sans Loy: Sans Joy:	Moslem power seen by Spenser to be naturally in league with Catholicism

Night:	the Old Law, in contrast to the New Law, which the Red Crosse Knight is to realise
Fauns and the satyrs:	uninformed instinct
Sir Satyrane:	said to be modelled upon Sir John Perrott, natural son of Henry VIII
Orgoglio:	Philip II of Spain
Arthur:	England, English strength and spirit (but also grace)
Dragon:	the Catholic Church

These are the main historical meanings to be attached to the allegory, but it must be emphasised that the significance of any one of these characters cannot be confined to its historical topicality: Spenser's method is not mechanically consistent. Each of these figures acquires further and more extensive resonances as the world of the narrative takes shape in the reader's mind.

Sources

Spenser's mind being so syncretic, it is not surprising to find that his sources are many. He draws upon the classical and contemporary European traditions of the epic (see the section on 'Kind', pp. 43-4), but he also draws considerably on native tradition. The choice of Arthur as the hero of the whole poem, who intervenes in the adventures of each knight, is a deliberately English choice, and was influenced by the *Morte d'Arthur* (printed 1485) of Sir Thomas Malory (*d.*1471) because Spenser wanted to ground his epic, for patriotic and religious reasons, in the soil of England.

The Red Crosse Knight, too, turns out to be St George, whose function, after his death, will be to guard the realm of England, and to maintain its devotion to Truth and unity. George means earth (from the Greek *georgos*), the earth of England, and he is associated with the ploughman, who turns the earth to bring forth new life. William Langland's fourteenth-century medieval poem, *Piers Plowman* (a vision of the state of the world in which Piers the ploughman offers to guide all those who are confused if they will work with him), was one of Spenser's sources and Piers certainly does stand behind Spenser's St George.

Each of the twelve books of the *Faerie Queene* (of which six and part of a seventh survive) was assigned a virtue, and these virtues were based on the Greek philosopher Aristotle's (384-322BC) *Nicomachean Ethics*. Ovid (43BC-AD17) is also a source, as well as Seneca (5BC-65AD) and Cicero (106-43BC) and Horace (65-8BC).

A source for one aspect of Spenser's allegorical method was the medieval and Tudor pageant. In this a procession of figures came before an audience, each one adding to the meaning as he or she came on. This tradition, which gave rise to the morality play and to the court masque, also had an effect on Spenser. The method whereby a series of figures emerged and declared their significance, wearing appropriate costumes, appealed to Spenser's visual and moralising imagination. It also involved the onlooker morally, in the same way that Spenser wished to draw his reader to realise his own moral nature by reflecting on the figures Spenser's pictures evoked in his mind, and by making him think of their relevance for his own spiritual state. This 'inward touch' (a phrase of Sir Philip Sidney's (1554-86), who was a patron of Spenser, and a writer with Puritan leanings) was something for which Spenser continually strove. It did not matter to him what the sources of his material were as long as he could make his reader really to read his poem. The word 'read' itself, in the sense of decipher, understand, fully apprehend, is one that Spenser uses time and again. The reader should be on the look-out for it.

Spenser's chief source, the one he comes back to unceasingly, so much so that there is hardly a single stanza which is not marked by its influence, is, of course, the Bible itself, particularly, in Book I, the Revelation of St John. If we look at the figure of the Red Crosse Knight, and how Spenser develops our conception of him in the narrative, we can form some idea both of Spenser's allegorical method in practice, and of his use of the Bible in such a way as to make his readers respond afresh to the meanings.

The moral allegory and the narrative

The Red Crosse Knight is in search of Holinesse, the virtue that is the basis for all others, and through which man comes to knowledge of, and eventual union with, Truth, here represented by Una. Her very name foretells the unity that is to come.

Something of Spenser's Puritanism can be seen in the way he opens the story of the Knight. The Knight is at first a lowly churl, who comes in shabby clothes to the court of the Faerie Queene. Una's armour fits him, so that he is chosen by Truth; he does not choose her. This emphasises the force of good; the Knight is one of the elect destined by God to achieve his full potential. It is by no means easy; he has to struggle through a great deal before he has the strength to take on the Dragon, and even that is only a preparation to fight the pagan king.

The poem itself opens in the middle of the action: the first stanza (which will repay close attention) is all energy and movement, with words such as 'angry', 'chide', 'foming bitt'. In the third stanza we are told of his foe, and the word 'foe' is used twice, to bring it home to us that he must defeat this foe, the Dragon, to learn his 'new force'. This new force comes with the role he has undertaken: to be a soldier of Christ, to go out into the adventurous world of chance, and test himself. Una, the lady whose champion he is, is with him.

Soon, the sky darkening, they go into a wood, a 'wandering wood', where Error has his cave. The wood for Spenser is that which is unknown and dangerous, but which has to be explored and searched, its dangers faced. Una names the place as Error's wood in stanza 13, appropriately enough, since thirteen is commonly regarded as an unlucky number. This is an unlucky place for the Red Crosse Knight. Una's dwarf, who is wise and commonsensical, says that the wood is not a place for living men: those who are half-living, who have surrendered their 'force', fall foul of Error.

When we are shown Error it is quite clear from the description that Spenser gives us, that here we encounter a first version of the Dragon the Knight is to fight at the end. Satan takes many forms, and this is his first disguise. Error has a thousand 'young ones' feeding on her in the dark cave. She entangles the Knight in her complexity (Spenser is thinking here of the subtleties of Roman Catholic theology and controversy), and when he 'knits all his force' (19) to grip her by the gorge, she spews up all kinds of books and pamphlets, the wrong kind of reading, clearly. The Knight escapes this complexity, darkness, and filth, and having killed Error, he makes his way with Una out of the forest quite easily.

Una is contrasted here with Error. Una is single and full of light; Error is multiple, complex and her environment is the dark. Error's reptilian fertility, her revolting young, contrast with the chastity of Una and her restraint. But the Red Crosse Knight is not immune from Error; he becomes entangled with her in the fight, which anticipates what is to happen to him later in his adventures, before he is given the vision of the pure light of Truth at the end of Book I, when Una is betrothed to him. The light, in the words of St John, is the 'life of men', it 'shineth in the darkness'; and it is the word of God (John 1). So Una is simple, true, and clear; and she is related to Christ's presence in the world. She is the free church as it exists in the material world, and the Knight's quest is for this to be revealed to him. Continuously we find him trapped or imprisoned in dark places underground, or slipping in the mire, until he is baptised at the end into the new 'force' of himself. In this way we can see Spenser weaving his narrative, and the different stories therein, in such a way as to bring out, explore, and realise the meanings of Revelation for man in this world. This is how the moral allegory works. The stories enact and thereby discover meanings in order that they may be carried living into the heart and there 'fashion' the new kind of man it is Spenser's aim to make the reader discover in himself. Reading, in Spenser, means being aware of moral implication, watchfulness. In the curious stanza 13 of Canto I, when Una identifies the place to which they have come as *Errours den* (the spelling of Errour here is no accidental archaism: Spenser wants us to read that this is *our* Error, that we are the Knight, that reading itself is a quest), she says 'Therefore I read beware'—where 'read' means 'warn' while carrying with it the more ordinary sense as well. To read is to be warned. The intricacy of Spenser's art, its attention to detail, is very elaborate; but again, it should be observed that his basic idea is very simple: the Knight is on the quest for union with the Truth of God.

Truth is simple and one. Evil is complicated and double. As soon as they come out of Error's wood they meet Archimago, in whom the Pope is represented, as well as much else. He *appears* to be a hermit, with a Bible at his belt. So, unlike Una, Archimago is double: he is evil, but he appears to be something else. He is now about to draw them both into another tangle of Error, but this time erotic, not doctrinal. His hermitage is, ominously, 'Downe in a dale, hard by a forest's side' which sounds pleasant, but it belongs to the world below if it is 'downe'. The first meaning of 'hard' in the context is 'near'; but we know already that forests are not good places for knights to find themselves in, so that 'hard' also conveys overtones of cruelty and difficulty. It is going to be hard for them here. (Throughout the poem Spenser's word-play is used like this, to draw the reader's attention to the meanings that are unfolding in the story.)

Archimago, it turns out, is a good talker, and spikes his conversation with many devout invocations of the Virgin Mary, but night comes on and they retire. It is at night that Archimago's true nature emerges. He is a magician, an expert at illusion, as has already been made clear, and he conjures up spirits, one of which fetches an 'ydle dreame' (46) for the Knight, in which Una seems to lie with him. His heart bathes in 'wanton blis', wallowing in lewdness, which contrasts with the strange baptism that takes place at the end of the book during his fight with the Dragon. The other spirit becomes a double of Una (again emphasising false doubles as against true simplicity). The Knight starts up from his delusion, only to encounter the illusion of Una before him, who has come to his bed. He resists her, but he is troubled and confused, his thoughts filled with images of abandon (55).

Archimago, the false creator who traffics in illusion, or 'miscreant' (a favourite word of Spenser's), shapes out of the Knight's dream a youth, whom he orders to couple with the false Una. He wakes the Knight up to come and see them in the act of love-making, which appals and torments him, and makes him 'Yrkesome of life' (II.6). He has, as A. C. Hamilton points out in his commentary (see Part 5,

Suggestions for further reading), begun his journey to Despair, brought upon him by 'subtill' Archimago. He leaves Una, thereby drawing away from her and venturing into illusion and doubleness. They are 'divided into double parts' (II.9).

To correspond with this, Archimago makes himself into a double of the Red Crosse Knight. The Knight himself now enters on the long series of encounters with the pagan knights, Sans Foy, Sans Loy and Sans Joy, who as faithlessness, betrayal, and misery, embody what he has become. Often we find this with Spenser: that the figures or places that a knight encounters are in fact externalisations of the condition to which he has become susceptible. But the most emphatic revelation of his condition is in the woman who is escorted by the first of these pagan knights, appropriately called Duessa, after all the doublings of what was originally single in the previous canto. She is Mary Tudor, but she is also the duplicity of the faithlessness that is her knight (Sans Foy). She pretends, of course, that she is true and faithful, and that her name is Fidessa. Her name means 'double being' and is also related to the Irish 'do-bhéas' which means 'evil custom'. This Irish dimension to Duessa is appropriate when it is remembered that the Irish in the sixteenth century often thought of themselves as waging a holy war against the English. Needless to say, the English thought the same about their wars against the Irish. The double vision, it may be said, has not even yet disappeared from Anglo-Irish relations.

At any rate, in Spenser, the plot thickens. Now we have false faith and false Holinesse at large. The moral implications of the story are clear: to divide from the path of truth is to enter a labyrinth.

The story of Fradubio (meaning 'in doubt') corresponds to that of the Red Crosse Knight: he and his lady, Fraelissa, are now separate, divided, in the form of two trees, under which the Knight and Duessa sit as they hear the tale that one of the trees tells. Duessa, appropriately, has been the cause of their division. They are to stay in this doubled state until they bathe in the water of life, which refers forward to the baptism of the Knight in his fight with the Dragon.

Duessa leads the Red Crosse Knight to the House of Pride, which, impressive though it is, is also a false appearance, because it is built on insecure foundations (IV.5). Enamoured of her brightness ('that too exceeding shone', IV.8), Lucifera holds up a mirror to look at her own 'selfe-lou'd substance' (IV.10), in direct contrast with Una, whose brightness is the light that darkness cannot grasp, the light of St John and of Revelation. This brightness in the House of Pride is the brightness of Lucifer, and, again, it is doubled in Pride's mirror. The House of Pride is a 'sad house' (V.53) and appropriately enough it is here that Sans Joy the pagan comes, to be defeated by the Red Crosse Knight. From here also Duessa takes the journey to Night, her original darkness, and together they persaude Aesculapius to heal Sans Joy. In Hades all the sadness and misery of the Classical after-life is evoked; all the hopelessness of its system where God's mercy does not intervene, where Christ's grace is unknown. It is an accursed place. The healing of Sans Joy by Aesculapius is to be contrasted with the healing of the Knight in the House of Holinesse later in the book.

The Red Crosse Knight leaves the House of Pride. On his way out by a back door in the great palace he passes through a dump full of unburied corpses laid up in heaps. This is the other side of Lucifera: her majesty and beauty hide filth and sadness.

Pride, it is said, comes before a fall, and now the Red Crosse Knight is truly to fall. Duessa (who has followed him) and he lie 'downe' (VII.6) together by a fountain's side. We may think of the water of life, but this water is against life, and saps his 'manly forces' (VII.6). He and she are 'pourd out in loosnesse on the grassy ground' (VII.7), and he, not thinking of his health or his fame, is making love to Duessa when the giant Orgoglio comes to confront him. His armour off, he is unready, and the giant defeats him and throws him into a 'Dongeon deepe' (VII.15) where 'dongeon' carries with it the suggestion of dung (spelt 'dong' in the description of the waste behind the House of Pride); and the 'deepe' suggests the depth of sin into which he has fallen.

Orgoglio is the gigantic might of Catholicism embodied in Philip II of Spain, but he is also the inflated pride of male sexual excitement and self-indulgence to which we see the Red Crosse Knight falling victim beside the enervating fountain. Orgoglio takes Duessa as his mistress and decks her out in all the finery of false pomp, including the 'triple crowne' of Papacy (VII.16). She is then revealed as the Whore of Babylon of the Book of Revelation, and he sets her to ride upon the great beast that he has kept in darkness waiting for her. In the Renaissance the Whore of Babylon was commonly identified with the Catholic Church in its corruption.

Arthur now enters the poem at this critical moment, to rescue the fallen knight. Arthur is grace and heavenly intervention. He does not solve everything but he comes in when he is most needed. His armour shines like the sun, linking him with Una, who is often related to the sun as well.

When the Red Crosse Knight is released he is shrunk and withered, his manhood all consumed; he has been robbed of his 'selfe' (VIII.42), as Una says to him, in the dark pit of Orgoglio's 'dongeon'. Duessa is stripped of her finery, and stands revealed in all her filth, her fox's tail 'with dong all fowly dight' (48).

The Red Crosse Knight, through Arthur's intervention, and through the unremitting concern of Una, has at last seen the ugliness of Duessa: she has been revealed to him, as in Revelation 17:8 where it is promised that all hidden corruption will in the end be made plain. We can see that this reflects a strong apocalyptic strain in Spenser's thought, and in the thought of his time. There was a longing for all duplicity to be swept away, and for things to be revealed in their stark simplicity: there was, in the terms of Spenser's poem, a yearning for Una. The radical thought of all ages tends to have this kind of apocalyptic strain: it is there in William Blake (who admired Spenser and did an engraving of him) and later in D.H. Lawrence (1885-1930).

Arthur is a figure out of British legend and it is appropriate that he should come to the aid of the Red Crosse Knight, who is destined to be St George of England when he attains his selfhood. To a certain extent we can see a historical strain operating on the moral and psychological allegory here, in that Arthur could be linked to the English Church: when Una sees him first his armour shines brilliantly, linking him with her, her sun imagery, and with the free Church of Christ, the Church of England under Elizabeth I. Again, the interpretations ramify, but the meaning is simple: Arthur and Una have much in common—Englishness, light, grace, and truth.

The Red Crosse Knight has defeated Error; he has escaped from the House of Pride and Orgoglio's castle; and he has seen Duessa for what she is. But he is still fallen from grace. Arthur will not solve everything for him. He must go through more trials and test himself to the last, though he carries with him Arthur's gift of Christ's blood in a 'boxe of Diamond' (IX.19), which is the blood of the 'new Testament, which is shed for many for the remission of sins' (Matthew 26:28).

Now, however, comes the subtlest temptation of all, and it is right that it should come *after* he has been given the promise of the blood of Christ. The temptation is that of Despair. Despair has brought Sir Terwin (Weariness) to such a pitch of despair that he has taken his own life, and the Red Crosse Knight demands he pay for it with his own blood. He is appalled by the 'sight' (IX.37), not grasping the fact that Despair is a sin of the individual soul, for which the self alone is guilty. Despair indeed is a denial of the value of self; it is the sense of exclusion from God's grace and mercy; and a reduction of life to what we can see with our limited vision. God's ways go beyond ours, but the Knight does not 'see' that; all he sees is the dead man in his blood and the figure of Despair. Despair, he says, must pay with his blood for the blood of this youth at his feet and immediately we see what has happened. He has forgotten about the blood of the New Testament, which Christ has shed, and which Arthur has given him; instead he only sees what is before him, and goes back to the law of the Old Testament—blood for blood. He is deceived; already he is in despair. It is easy for Despair to win him over. The Knight argues against suicide, but in such a way as to lead himself to despair. Indeed, Spenser deliberately arranges the argument here (IX.41-7) so as to make it uncertain who says what, the point being that Despair is now the Knight, the Knight Despair. Again, the basic idea is remarkably simple: the Knight says that our time is allotted to us, and Despair picks up his words and turns them into an argument about Fate—that we are wretched and unable to do anything for ourselves, therefore to die is best. It could be the Knight who says all this, and, in a certain sense, it is, since Despair has taken him over. Of God he asks:

Shall he thy sins up in his knowledge fold,
And guiltie be of thine impietie? (IX.47)

The answer to which, we know from the Matthew text already cited, is 'yes', because Christ's blood has been shed for the remission of sins. But again the Knight is taken in by what is laid before him. Despair (now called the 'Miscreant' (IX.49) or bad creator, as Archimago was) shows him a painting of the damned souls in hell, knowing full well that the Knight will succumb to visual proof, because he still believes totally in what he sees.

As he is on the point of taking his own life, Una is chilled to the core of her being (her 'well of life', IX.52) and awakens his faith by reminding him that he has been chosen to achieve himself and fight the Dragon of Satan.

Balanced now with the episode in which Duessa took Sans Joy to Hades to the infernal healer Aesculapius, is the section devoted to the renewal and strengthening of the Knight's faith in the House of Holinesse. After all the false starts and trials, a beginning is at last being made and once begun it all happens very easily.

Each goodly thing is hardest to begin,
  But entred in a spacious court they see,
  Both plaine, and pleasant to be walked in. (X.6)

These lines in their simplicity, and in the chastity of their diction, convey the nature of the house to which Una has brought the Knight.

Faith, Hope and Charity, in the persons of Fidelia, Speranza and Charissa, minister to the Knight, Faith appropriately coming first, as this is where the Knight requires most support, as we know from his tendency to Despair. Fidelia expounds the Bible (19) which is with 'blood ywrit', the blood of Christ, which Arthur gave the Knight to keep. Now the meaning of that blood is explained by Faith, which, in a sense, is what Spenser is trying to do in his poem. The words she speaks terrify and kill in their awesomeness, but unlike the words of Despair, they also raise the heart to life again, in a spiritual resurrection:

> For she was able, with her words to kill,
> And raise againe to life the hart, that she did thrill. (X.19)

No-one can 'read' this book, unless taught by her.

At the end of the course of instruction, healing, and discipline in the House of Holiness the Knight is brought to see the new Jerusalem that John saw in Revelation 21:2: 'And John saw the holy city, new Jerusalem, coming down from God out of Heaven, prepared as a bride adorned for her husband' (see all of X.57). This is the vision which the Red Crosse Knight and Una are destined to achieve. He is to be St George, the earthly holiness of England; she his true church. Dazzled with the brightness, his earthly eyes are darkened; but in the end he comes back to himself: 'himself he gan to find' (X.68), which applies to his quest as well. At last he has begun to find his true path. Now he is ready for the trial, the fight with the Dragon.

As a good story-teller should, Spenser has built up suspense in the reader, so that he is now very anxious to see if the Dragon is as terrifying as he has been made out to be. And he is. Spenser's description of him is a masterpiece. Full of detail, it represents the manifold nature of evil. Like pride, the Dragon shines with false glory—

> strecht he lay upon the sunny side
> Of a great hill, himselfe like a great hill. (XI.4)

The Dragon and the Knight fight. At the end of the first day Satan burns the Red Crosse Knight with a sheet of flame from the 'deuouring oven' of his stomach. But, where the Knight stands, 'vnweeting' (XI.29), the well of life flows, so that when he falls, it is a fortunate fall, into the water of life which has the property of restoring the dead to life, and of renewing those exhausted by 'long decay' (XI.30). This is the baptism of fire, in that his suffering at the hands of the Devil has thrown him into the well of God's mercy, where he will be renewed. This parallels and ratifies the other, false baptisms, of the earlier parts of the Book: his baptism in 'wanton blis' as he dreamed the delusive dream concocted by Archimago, and the enfeebling water that he drank with Duessa when they were 'pourd out' (VII.7) in abandonment on the ground before Orgoglio came and took him captive.

Spenser brilliantly conveys the effect of the Knight's increased grace by his description of the attack he makes on the Dragon the next morning, after he has arisen from the well, refreshed. He says that he does not know whether the steel of the Knight's sword was hardened with holy water; or whether it developed a sharper edge; or whether his hands were just stronger:

I wote not whether the revenging steele
  Were hardened with that holy water dew,
  Wherein he fell, or sharper edge did feele,
  Or his baptized hands now greater grew;
  Or other secret vertue did ensue (XL.36).

He does not (and probably Spenser would argue that no man can) commit himself as to what happens; God's grace is not to be understood in our terms, but we can feel it. And this is artfully suggested by rhyming 'feele' with 'steele'. It is as if the coming of grace can be felt like a harder edge to steel. The rhyme between 'dew' and 'grew' also suggests that the holy water of the Knight's baptism actually, in some kind of secret way, makes his hands grow. Certainly it makes them more capable, because now he really damages the Dragon: he brings the sword down onto its head with such force (XI.36) that it makes a deep wound down into the skull, smashing through the plating of brass and steel on its skin, which had never been broken through before. The new man, the man who is going to realise himself in the new Jerusalem, has arrived. The Knight is a totally Christian hero.

At the end of the second day of the conflict the Knight falls a second time, again brought down by the 'scorching fire' (XI.45) of the Dragon's breath. This time, near where he falls is the *tree of life* itself. This tree is the very tree from which Adam and Eve could not eat after they had broken God's commandment and eaten from the tree of knowledge. This tree of life reminds us that the fight is taking place in Eden for Eden: this was once Eden, but it now is under the sway of the Dragon who must be defeated by the Christian. The Christian, Red Crosse Knight, receives sustenance from the tree of life during the second night of his ordeal, and here we see that this tree is to be associated with Holy Communion, a sacrament, like the Baptism of the well of life. Holy Communion is the eating of the tree of life, which is Christ himself on the cross. It was an old tradition that the Cross of Calvary was placed in the same spot where the tree of life had stood in Eden. Again, we see that Spenser sees this world as a potential Eden; that the fruit of Paradise may be ours to eat if we fight the Dragon; that, in a word, Paradise may be regained through Holy Communion with Christ. Furthermore, the fact that the Knight happens to fall in just that place indicates that Spenser is trying to make his reader understand, feelingly, the watchfulness and care of God, shown in the presence of Christ. All Spenser's powers of luxuriant description are summoned to evoke the peace that the 'trickling streame of Balme' (XI.48) brings which flows from the tree. This is the blood of Christ that poured from his side when he was crucified, and into this the Knight falls, so that he is 'Besmeared with pretious Balme' (XI.50).

On the third day he arises, again refreshed. The three-day fight with the forces of darkness parallels the three days Christ spent in the Harrowing of Hell after his death on Good Friday. The Knight rises, like Christ, on the third day and very quickly vanquishes the Dragon. Spenser makes the point that it is the weapon which does the final killing, again emphasising that it is God's grace which gives the Knight his force (XI.53).

At the feast at which the Red Crosse Knight and Una are to be promised to each other, Archimago arrives, bringing a letter from Duessa, claiming the Knight as her own. Even here, in the midst of the solemn feasts of Eden, even in the midst of the communion which the Knight and his lady are to enjoy, duplicity enters. But the deception is quickly exposed, and the betrothal ceremonies proceed. Interwoven with the music of the feast is a 'heavenly noise', so that each one in the hall feels himself 'secretly' (XII.39) lifted up out of himself, and his spirit 'ravished' with an impression of pure joy and loveliness and union. It is a fitting end to a Book concerned with the search for the joyous union with what is true.

The quest for Holinesse

All knights go on quests in search of truth. The Red Crosse Knight's search is for union with Truth, represented in the figure of Una. In searching for that union he is in search of Holinesse. Therefore the Red Crosse Knight is the Knight of Holinesse in that it is Holinesse to which he is devoted, and to which his whole being aspires. When he comes to the House of Holinesse he is coming home to his rightful place, to that place of simplicity, hope, and love to which he belongs. Fortified by that homecoming and by his victory over Despair he can face the Dragon. This, Spenser would have his reader understand, is the pattern of a holy life.

The other figures in the story

The roles of all the other figures in the story can be understood by studying their places in the allegory of the Red Crosse Knight's adventures. The main points about them may be summarised here.

Una

Una is truth, and she is also to be associated with Elizabeth I, and with the Church of England. As long as she is with him the Red Crosse Knight cannot come to much harm. England is protected once she holds sway; its strength, its St George quality, is safe. However, he can be separated from her through the artfulness and guile of Archimago, who creates a false Una the sight of whom deceives the Knight (he is very quickly taken in by appearances). He leaves her in Archimago's hermitage, thinking she is morally loose, and immediately, without her, encounters Sans Foy and Duessa. Sans Foy means 'without faith', which describes the Knight's condition now that he is without Una, and Duessa is another false Una. Indeed the name she often uses is that of faith itself, Fidessa.

Una is protected by the lion of England, a kind of Red Crosse Knight himself, who can be associated with Henry VIII, in whose reign the Protestant Reformation came to England. Archimago, who by now has assumed the guise of the Red Crosse Knight, seeks her out, Sans Loy overcomes Archimago and kills the lion. Lucifera, Pride, is another false Una.

The fauns and satyrs rescue Una from Sans Loy, and their instinctive nature recognises her goodness. They represent the primitive in man and nature, that longs for coherence, harmony, and security, which they can see she embodies.

Sir Satyrane, a knight who has a strong element of brutishness in him, but who is courageous and noble also, leads Una out of the wild wood. They meet Archimago, who tells them her knight is dead.

By now the real Red Crosse Knight is a prisoner at the Castle of Orgoglio, to which Una now goes. On the way she meets Arthur, who has much in common with her. He, like her, is associated with the sun, with light, and with truth.

When the Red Crosse Knight is released from Orgoglio's castle, Duessa, in Una's presence, is stripped of her finery and she stands revealed as she really is, the Whore of Babylon, and the description of her at this point (VIII.48) is modelled on the Book of Revelation. It is appropriate that she should be stripped of all her disguises in Una's presence: this is the first time that they have encountered each other. Duplicity must be revealed for what it is in the presence of truth. Again, the thought is simple, but it is Spenser's art to convey the strength of the thought, freshly realised in the narrative.

The Knight falls into Despair, but Una rescues him by reminding him that he has a part in 'heavenly mercies' (IX.53). Knowing that he is weak, she brings him to the House of Holinesse, where he is healed for the fight with the Dragon.

During the fight, she is apart, 'aloofe' (XI.5), indicating that in the final struggle with the Devil, man is alone, though he may be helped by the intervention of grace (the well of life, the tree of life).

At the end, Una is betrothed to her Knight. She is described as 'faire and fresh, as freshest flowre in May' (XII.22); the 'glorious light of her sunshyny face' (XII.23) is revealed to the Knight. He sees her as she really is, the Truth of Christ in his Church, 'a woman clothed with the sun' (Revelation 12:1).

Duessa

Where Una is fair and simple and true, Duessa is ugly and complicated and false. She, like Archimago, is an expert at disguise. Where Una is associated with light, Duessa is linked with darkness.

As soon as her Knight leaves Una, under a misapprehension, he meets Duessa, doubleness. In the story within a story about Fradubio and Fraelissa in Canto II (appropriately the canto in which she appears, as her nature is double) we learn how she divides her victims from those they love and from what they themselves should be in order to be complete persons. She parts Fradubio (whose story 'doubles' or mirrors that of the Knight) from Fraelissa, by making him believe that what she tells him is true. When he finds out the truth about Duessa, seeing her horrible awfulness as she bathes one day, it is too late, and, already under her spell, he is further reduced to a sub-human state by her magic arts. Now he and his love are near each other, but, degraded to trees by his weakness, they await a baptism that will renew them, and lift them out of their sin. This water which will renew Fradubio and Fraelissa points forward to the well of life in Canto XI.

Duessa, following her inclinations, leads the Knight to the House of Pride, with the mistress of which she has many affinities: in Pride's house, she gets as close as she can to Lucifera. All this time her falseness is at work, pretending she is faithful and true and that her name is Fidessa. In the joust between the Red Crosse Knight and Sans Joy she pretends to be true to the former, while secretly favouring the latter. When Sans Joy is defeated, she covers him with an enchanted cloud (she is linked with the dark and disguise), until she can bring him, with the aid of Night, to Hades, where he may be healed by infernal medicine, or black arts. Notice that this knight is called, appropriately, Sans Joy, without Joy. This is the misery, Spenser would have his reader realise, that is the true condition of falseness and scheming.

The Red Crosse Knight's quest is to find his new self, to become the new man in Christ, to be baptised. Duessa leads him to a false baptism by a fountain-side. Drinking from this stream his 'manly forces gan to faile' (VII.6) so that he is overcome by Orgoglio, who sits Duessa on the beast of Revelation. When Arthur comes to defeat Orgoglio, Duessa tries to thwart him, but fails. When Orgoglio is killed she is stripped of her garments and her foulness is revealed.

She does not completely disappear, however. At the end of the Book she sends Archimago to the ceremony of betrothal in Eden, claiming that the Knight is promised to her. He had, indeed, compromised himself, but now, with the strength given to him by God, and awakened by Una, he may go forward, leaving that association behind.

Archimago

Archimago is an arch-magician, as his name implies. His is, however, a false and delusive creativity. He is an artist, but a black one, in that he uses his creative powers to lead virtue astray. His is the opposite of the kind of art Spenser wants to practise, since Spenser wants to show, by example, how Truth may be discovered.

He is a master of disguise. He can assume the likeness of a hermit, of the Red Crosse Knight himself, and of the messenger at the end of the Book. He is a story-teller, in that he invents fictions so as to entrap people. He tells Una that he has seen the Red Crosse Knight killed, and he tells this lie in order to drive her to despair, and because he wishes to destroy the unity and simplicity of Truth.

He is very quick with his answers. In VI.39, for instance, when he tells Una that her knight is slain, she exclaims:

> Ah dearest Lord (quoth she) how might that bee,
> And he the stoutest knight, that euer wonne?

At which he comes back, immediately, mimicking the style of her speech exactly, picking up the tone of her grief, and giving it back to her in a mirror image:

> Ah dearest dame (quoth he) how might I see
> The thing, that might not be, and yet was donne?

A reader will probably feel that the character of Iago in Shakespeare's *Othello* (1604) owes something to the trickery and artfulness of Archimago. The names, too, have a certain suggestive similarity.

The paynim knights

Sans Foy, Sans Joy and Sans Loy are the opposite of the trinity of the virtues: Faith, Hope and Charity. Sans Foy is first seen with Duessa; Sans Loy attacks Una and kills the lion who is her protector; and Sans Joy appears at the House of Pride.

Orgoglio

Linked with Philip II of Spain in the historical allegory, he is the giant who comes to the Red Crosse Knight when he lies in dalliance with Duessa by the enervating fountain in Canto VII. Three times the normal human size, he stands for male lust and sexual pride. It is not surprising that he carries a great snaggy club with him, which he has torn out of the bowels of his mother, who is the earth. There is something ludicrous about this giant, bellowing his way through the forest, all puffed up with wind, but he is extremely dangerous as well. He puts the Red Crosse Knight into his 'dongeon', and takes Duessa for his 'deare' (VII.16), placing on her head the papal crown and setting her to ride upon the great beast he has kept a long time in his 'darksome den' (VII.16). When Arthur comes to challenge him he is found, appropriately, in dalliance with Duessa. In the fight, the veil slips from Arthur's shield and dazzles Orgoglio. When Arthur cuts off his head the giant disappears. There is nothing left of the 'monstrous man'; he is like an 'emptie bladder' (VIII.24). The reader should look at this stanza and study the rhymes, paying particular attention to the last two rhymes that end the stanza:

of that monstrous mas
Was nothing left, but like an emptie bladder was.

Here the rhyme joining 'mas' and 'was' emphasises that the giant's mass has vanished. This slight off-rhyme also brings out the element of the comic that surrounds Orgoglio. It used to be thought that Spenser was a very humourless poet: now that we understand his word play better we can see that he can often be witty in the way that this example shows.

Arthur

Arthur is England, English strength and English grace, so that he has a special relationship with the Red Crosse Knight, whose destiny is to become St George in the new Jerusalem, watching over England, as her 'Patrone' saint (X.61). It is through Arthur's assistance that he gains this vision of his destiny, because, had Arthur not intervened, he should not have escaped from the Castle of Orgoglio.

Arthur is magnificence, Spenser tells us in the letter to Raleigh (see p. 17), 'which virtue is the perfection of all the rest'. His intervention in Book I helps the Knight to achieve his end, as it does all the knights in the other books.

Arthur enters the story in Canto VII, when the Red Crosse Knight has been thrown into Orgoglio's 'dongeon', and Una is stricken with grief at the loss of her Knight. His armour is described in full: he carries a shield hewn out of a diamond, which he keeps covered, except when the odds against him are unnaturally powerful. The shield is extraordinarily bright and no magic can have any power over it. Everything that is false is revealed in its true form when the shield is unveiled. It is a symbol of truth, of the light that shines in the darkness, and so it is linked with Una, who is also associated with truth and light. Spenser also says that the Faerie Queene (Elizabeth) brought it to England when Arthur died, and that it can still be seen there 'if sought' (VII.36). This shield will remain in England forever, Spenser is implying; it can be discovered if the will is there. His ambition is obviously to arouse his reader by this thought, that he might be exercised to awaken the will to see Arthur's shield for himself, in himself.

Arthur's first task is to raise Una's spirits. The beginning of their exchange (VII.41) is an exact parallel of the exchange between Una and Archimago at VI.39:

> O but (quoth she) great griefe will not be tould
>   And can more easily be thought than said. (VII.41)

But Arthur, instead of picking up her tone and rhythm, and giving back to her a mirror-image, a doubling of her own mind (as Archimago had), breaks up the dreary regularity of her syntax, and throws all her predictable rhythms into disarray, challenging her will and her mind:

> Right so; (quoth he) but he, that never would,
> Could never: will to might gives greatest aid.

Get up, he is saying; do not languish; you have to try, and trying strengthens. His reasoning 'So deepe did settle in her gratious thought' (VII.42)—her thought is now beginning to be 'gratious' again, because Arthur has renewed her grace—that she tells him about herself, her parents, the Dragon, and the present captivity of the Knight through the wiles of Duessa.

Arthur and his squire challenge Orgoglio, summoning the giant out of his dalliance with Duessa by a bugle, the sound of which is linked to the sound of the last trumpet on the Day of Judgement, the day of apocalypse. Orgoglio's castle quakes

>   from the ground
> And every dore of freewill open flew. (VIII.5)

(The reader should always pay attention to the minute details of Spenser's verse: here 'freewill' is charged with meaning—Arthur brings 'freewill' into the captivity of spirit that the love-making of Orgoglio and Duessa embodies.) So strong is the sound that it smashes open the door, exposing them to the energy of Arthur's just rage. In the fight that follows, Orgoglio knocks Arthur down, but as he falls the shield is uncovered, and its 'blazing brightnesse through the aier threw' (VIII.19), dazzling the giant and his beast, on which Duessa rides. The shield is 'sunshiny' (VIII.20), the same word that Spenser uses in XII.23 to describe the 'blazing brightnesse' (again the same words) of Una's face. The sun is one, the lord of the planets, and linked with Justice. The victory of light over darkness is represented in Arthur's victory over Orgoglio and the beast; and, Spenser would say, in it is foretold the victory of the Knight over the Dragon.

Inside Orgoglio's castle, Arthur comes upon the horrible sight of a great room the floor of which is covered with the blood of innocents, drenched in the blood of martyred saints. (Very possibly Spenser is thinking of the St Bartholomew's Day Massacre here.) At last he comes to the Red Crosse Knight's 'dongeon', the door of which he rends 'with furious force' (VIII.39). He brings the Knight out, exhausted, starved, and 'shronk' (VIII.41).

Having stripped Duessa, and banished her, Arthur tells Una and her knight of his quest. He was taken from his human parents and reared in Faerie Land. One day in a dream the Queen of Faeries came to him and he fell in love with her. Now it is his quest to seek her. We learn that she is Gloriana, and that the idea of Arthur seeking to find her is linked to the return of the spirit of Arthur to Elizabeth I herself. Arthur, the grace of England, is trying to bring about a union with the Faerie Queene, who is also the Queen of England herself in Spenser's poem. Before they part, he and the Red Crosse Knight exchange gifts: Arthur gives a box of diamond containing a few drops of a miraculous liquid (Christ's blood, the elixir of life); the Knight gives a New Testament.

Structure

The structure of a work of art is the principle that gives it its coherence. What are the features of a work of literature that give it shape and that contribute to its overall meaning and impact? Once we identify these we find the structure. If a work of art is fully realised it will have a structure; if not, it will not.

What is the single strongest unifying element in Book I of *The Faerie Queene*? If we find that, we can start to develop a discussion of its structure. By now it should be clear what this unifying element is. It is the idea of Oneness: Truth is one; falsehood is double. It is, of course, entirely deliberate that Book I should deal with the theme of unity. The Knight is to be one with Una, whose name itself means 'one'. Her brightness is symbolised by light, which proceeds from one source, the sun. The forest, in which so much happens, is a place where that light grows diffuse and darkens; and where the travellers, who seek the light, may be led astray, as the Red Crosse Knight is almost immediately, by Archimago. And very soon night comes on, when soft delusions trouble the sleep and evil can work its will. Una's double is created in the night, falsifying the oneness of truth. Duessa is introduced, whose nature is entirely double. Even when Archimago speaks to Una (VI.39) he doubles her speech, giving back a mirror of her own despair.

To stay true to the truth, the one, one must stay true to oneself. Despair gains power over the Knight in his weakness, and the Knight loses himself so that he becomes indistinguishable from Despair. He *is* Despair, no longer the Red Crosse Knight.

To be one with truth is to be oneself, to be standing in grace. A list of concepts associated with oneness can be compiled, and a corresponding list of concepts associated with doubleness or duplicity:

Truth	Falsehood
Una	Duessa
Light	Dark
Arthur	Orgoglio
Caelia	Lucifera
House of Holiness	House of Pride, Archimago's hermitage
Fidelia (Faith)	Sans Foy
Speranza (Hope)	Sans Joy
Charissa (Charity)	Sans Loy
Well of Life	The enfeebling fountain
Tree of Life	Fradubio and Fraelissa
Reason	Dreams
Will	Despair
Jerusalem	House of Pride, Orgoglio's Castle, Eden under the Dragon
Lion	Beast
Ceremony	Disorder

The reader will have noticed that Spenser sets up deliberate comparisons: the fountain from which the Knight drinks before dallying with Duessa is recalled by the well of life into which he falls during his fight with the Dragon. The contrast between both is obvious and its meaning quite plain. There are other examples of episodes or images which parallel one another. The list above will help the reader to extract these for himself.

The unifying principle is oneness. The pattern by means of which this unity is expressed is the pattern of Christian redemption: man has fallen from his original unity (the Dragon is in Eden); he searches for Truth (Una), however, and Truth searches for him. After many trials he sees his heavenly destiny (Jerusalem), and defeats the Dragon, through the grace of Christ (Arthur, the tree of life), and the power of the Holy Spirit (Una, the well of life). The pattern is entirely traditional.

Another aspect of the pattern is that it takes the form of a journey, the traditional form of the search for truth in literature and story-telling. And as well as being a serious moralist, Spenser is a great story-teller. His descriptions, as well as contributing to the emotional and moral depth of the poem, are interesting and captivating in themselves.

The Spenserian stanza and Spenser's language

His stanza is Spenser's great contribution to English metric system. It consists of nine lines with five beats in each line, save the last, which has six beats. Another way of putting this is to say that there are eight pentameters and one alexandrine. The first and third lines rhyme, as do the second, fourth, fifth and seventh. Lines six, eight, and nine also rhyme. The following is a description of the House of Pride (IV.5):

It was a goodly heape for to behould, *a*
And spake the praises of the workman's wit; *b*
But full great pittie that so faire a mould *a*
Did on so weake foundation ever sit: *b*
For on a sandie hill, that still did flit, *b*
And fall away, it mounted was full hie, *c*
That every breath of heaven shaked it: *b*
And all the hinder parts, that few could spie, *c*
Were ruinous and old, but painted cunningly. *c*

The rhymes interlace, the new one entering in line 6, but the previous one is used again (in line 7) as a prelude to the couplet that concludes the stanza, recalling the couplet of lines 4 and 5. The alexandrine that concludes, being longer, urges the reader on towards the next stanza, the next phase of the narrative unfolding.

Something may be said here of the artistry of Spenser's technique. This has been referred to throughout, but the reader should try to summarise his thoughts on Spenser's metrical and linguistic skill at this stage.

The House of Pride is a 'goodly heape', but we should be warned about things which are 'goodly': it is a slightly silly-sounding word, with a sense of triviality about it. Further, Duessa has been described as a 'goodly lady' in II.13, and we have seen what she is like. Also, the fact that this 'heape' (a word implying confusion, though it can be used for a building), 'spake the praises of the workman's wit' should put us on our guard—it is a showy place, where the workman who made it was allowed free play to indulge his 'wit'. Now 'wit' is rhymed with 'sit' and 'flit': this work of wit was built upon sandy foundations, so where it sits it flits. Again, the sense of humour coming out in these rhymes, is linked to a judgement that is forming gradually as the writing proceeds. It is a 'full great pittie' that this 'mould' of pride (there is an indirect reference to man here: man was moulded out of clay) should be so unstable as to flit on its foundation. The word 'flit' is brilliantly chosen, suggesting, as it does, fractional movement, and the sense of something flitting away. As the stanza moves into its second phase this 'flitting' falls away, just as a heap of sand, after falling slightly, will suddenly collapse. The rhythm enacts and presents that realisation, and gives it a moral focus:

For on a sandie hill, that still did flit,
And fall away . . .

There is a suddenness in the new line; the rhythm opens and lengthens. This 'sandie hill' refers, of course, to the famous passage in the Gospel of St Matthew about the foolish man who built his house upon sand (Matthew 7:26-7). All the hinder parts of the house are in ruin, just as Duessa, when stripped of her clothes, is shown to be ugly, filthy and foul, especially in her lower parts (see VIII.48). The rhyme between 'spie' and 'cunningly', in the contrast between the length of 'cunningly' and the brevity of 'spie', suggests the complexity and cunning of Pride, which are so often so difficult to see in others, and in ourselves. We, Spenser is saying, keep the hinder parts well disguised, well painted over. That is our elaborate cunning that is so difficult to 'spie'.

From this it will be quite clear how Spenser's language and technique contribute to the effectiveness of the poem in fashioning its reader in 'vertuous and gentle discipline'. Spenser would say that it is a discipline for the reader to attend to the technique of his poem.

The archaism of Spenser's language sometimes attracts comment. It is true that no-one in his own time spoke the kind of English that

Spenser wrote, in all its particulars, but that is true of any writer. Where he differs from most other writers is in the degree of unusualness in his language. Old words from Chaucer and from dialect, and inventions of his own, all go to make up the variety and the oddness of his language. But there are reasons for this. He wanted to make as much use of the resources of English as he could, and so felt free to go back to medieval English literature for some of his words and spellings ('elfe' as a word for a knight, or 'sithens', since, and so on). Spenser was, we must remember, writing at a time when modern English literature was only beginning, and *The Faerie Queene* is a forceful assertion of the capability, dignity, flexibility and *age* of the language in which it is written.

However, beyond that, he wanted his reader to be ever-watchful of the words he was reading, so he could pick up the moral resonances being sounded in the details of the language. He wanted his reader to understand that this was not just an old language, but one charged with meanings which he could realise for himself.

Part 4

Hints for study

Points for detailed study

Allegory

The Faerie Queene is one of the most famous allegories in English, and students answering questions on the poem will find themselves frequently referring to allegory in one way or another. The allegorical method underlies everything else in the poem. Spenser wanted to write a story which would be of interest as a story, but he also wanted to exercise a moral influence upon his readers. Each episode in the story, then, has a meaning (or meanings) beyond the circumstances of the narrative, which involves the reader in considerations of right and wrong, self-examination and judgement. To read an allegory, Spenser would argue, is to use not just one's imaginative faculty, but one's understanding and conscience as well. This is why he wrote, in the letter to Raleigh, that he wanted 'to fashion a gentleman or noble person in vertuous and gentle discipline'. The student should thoroughly familiarise himself with every implication of that phrase, because questions on *The Faerie Queene* often make use of it. The whole letter to Raleigh should be read very carefully, because in it he sums up briefly the allegorical method. The student should re-read the section on allegory in Part 3 of these Notes, but the various salient points are summed up here:

1. Allegory is a 'darke conceit', or a story in which different levels of meaning operate together in a way that is not entirely obvious.
2. Allegory is a suitable method for writers with a strong sense of purpose. In Spenser's case it was a way of bringing religious and moral truths to the reader's understanding in a vivid and immediate way.
3. Allegory involves the reader, because all the meanings of a given episode are not immediately obvious, and he has to exercise his wit and intelligence in discovering for himself what the writer is trying to express in the story.
4. Spenser's allegory is not monovalent: that is, Una is not just Truth; she is also Elizabeth; she is the free church; and she is the source of the growth of faith in the individual soul. Spenserian allegory is polyvalent.

5. Spenser's allegory is linked to the people and politics of his own period. The artistic working out of the allegorical implications in Spenser's story is described in the section entitled 'The moral allegory and the narrative' in Part 3.

Theme

The theme of Book I is Holinesse. It is the virtue that the Red Crosse Knight is to embody; it is his destiny. Spenser's conception of Holinesse is not just simply dutiful devotion—that, as he indicates to us in the episode of Corceca and Kirkrapine, can be hypocritical, sad, and fearful. Spenser's House of Holinesse is connected with *wholeness*, with what it is to be a whole man, or woman. And that for Spenser means being true to oneself, keeping vigorously to the path on which things stand out firm and clear, and avoiding the forests of soft delusions and easy options. Needless to say, the Knight loses himself, leaving Una, Truth, oneness, wholeness, and goes off with doubleness herself, Duessa. Eventually he is released from the 'dongeon' (with the deliberate pun on 'dung') of Orgoglio's castle by Arthur, but he is exhausted and raw: 'His rawbone armes . . . were clene consumed' (VIII.41). He is shattered and tired because he has lost contact with himself and with the Truth, represented by Una. He has the desire to be whole, and he goes to be healed (a word connected with the words 'whole' and 'Holy'), to the House of Holinesse. After this he can see Jerusalem, and defeat the Dragon, because he has begun to be a complete man, a new man, a Christian.

There are other themes in the book, but they all contribute to this central idea and purpose.

Purpose

Any question on Spenser's purpose will mean that students will be involved in considering his moral aim and the allegorical method he adopted to achieve it.

Setting

Spenser's world is the world of Romance (knights, ladies, quests, castles, forests, dragons, dungeons, magic), but that world *moralised*. The forest is the 'forrest wilde', where a knight in quest of Holinesse may go astray, where nothing is necessarily what it seems. The House of Lucifera is the 'sad' house of Pride. The Dragon is Satan himself. The haven where the Knight rests and is healed is the House of Holinesse.

Spenser's setting is also the human mind, which contains Una *and* Duessa, Caelia *and* Lucifera, Jerusalem *and* Satan. Spenser's aim is to alert the reader that true virtue involves a battle between these forces. To be conscious is to be at war. This is what it is to be a soldier of Christ, a *miles Christi*. But Spenser's view of the mind is not one of unremitting conflict: he sees grace as playing an active part, as entering into the human struggle, to bring about a deeper order of harmony and delight. That delight is expressed in the last scene of the Book, which is set in Adam's house, when the heavenly music sounds (XII.39—which, incidentally, redeems the unlucky number 13, by multiplying it by 3, the number of the Trinity) and the knight looks upon his lady in full content and peace.

Contrast

Spenser makes continual use of contrast in order to clarify his purpose. Often these contrasts are stark and simple, but no less effective for that: Una is associated with sunlight, Duessa with the moon, magic, clouds, and darkness. A system of parallels underlies the moral design and the biblical material. For example, Fradubio and Fraelissa are separated into two trees, showing the sub-human state to which they have been reduced through Duessa's guile. Their story, told by one of the trees, is indeed the Red Crosse Knight's own story at that very moment: he too is separated from Una through guile. But these trees are paralleled and redeemed by the Tree of Life under which the Knight falls in his struggle with the Dragon. The balm which oozes from this tree is Christ's blood, because this tree is also the Cross which has redeemed mankind, and freed them from the captivity of their own weakness which brings them down from the human to something less than that. Parallels such as these contribute to the coherence of Spenser's work; they form part of its structure. (See the section on 'Structure' in Part 3 for further examples of contrasts and parallels.)

Style

Much has been written about the musical quality of Spenser's verse, all of which is true, but he can be harsh too. His style reflects and enacts the meaning: often it works as a physical realisation of a moral or emotional state. Study the irregularity of metre in XI.4.5-6, where the jumpiness and repetition convey the shock of seeing something as awful as the Dragon embodied in ourselves or others.

Another aspect of his style is his pictorial sense, which really is part of his allegorical method. He wants the reader to see a place (which will also be a state or a mood), by constructing it for himself in his own imagination, embroidering it in his own mind, guided by Spenser's description, and led by his interpretation.

Imagery

Spenser's imagery contributes to the pictures he gets his readers to construct in their minds. See previous section on Style.

Plot

Spenser's plot is utterly simple. The true knight, after many difficulties, comes to Eden, fights the Dragon, and defeats him. The figures and events that lead him astray contribute to the moral meaning: they are integral to the design. For example, when the Knight leaves Una (one) he has divided himself from the Truth, so he is split: therefore he meets Duessa (doubleness) who leads him, not a merry, but a sad dance, into her darkness. The Fradubio episode is not just a charming story copied from Ovid: it comments on the Knight's condition.

The Bible

The influence of the Bible is to be felt in virtually every stanza of Spenser's. In Book I, Revelation is ever present in much of the action. Una is the woman who flies from the beast; Duessa is the harlot who is stripped. Jerusalem is the wholeness that is Holinesse, to which the Knight aspires. But St John's *Gospel* is also there, especially in the light imagery, and the other Evangelists too. Genesis is there in the story of Adam and Eve (Una's parents), and Christ's redemption of mankind in the defeat of the Dragon.

Useful quotations

1. new force (I.3)

   The Knight must learn his 'new force' or energy. He is to find out what it is to be a new man, a man of the New Testament.

2. But subtill *Archimago*, when his guests
   He saw divided in double parts,
   And *Una* wandering in woods and forrests,
   Th' end of his drift . . . (II.9)

   Archimago has divided the Knight from Truth, into 'double parts'. Duessa is very soon to come upon the scene. This is his 'drift'.

3. He had a faire companion of his way,
   A goodly lady clad in scarlot red,
   Purfled with *gold* and pearle of rich assay,
   And like a *Persian* mitre on her hed
   She wore . . . (II.13)

The first entrance of Duessa, appropriately at Stanza 13 of Canto II. 'Goodly' is not a good word in Spenser: see the description of the House of Pride in IV.5; also the word 'scarlot' hides 'lot', with the suggestion of Lot's wife, as well as echoing 'harlot'. 'Purfled' means embroidered, but it also has a sense of being 'puffed-up'. She wears the mitre of the Papacy on her head.

4. And them beside
   Forth ryding underneath the castell wall,
   A donghill of dead carkases he spide,
  The dreadfull spectacle of that sad house of Pride. (V.53)

What the Knight and his dwarf see as they leave Lucifera's house.

5. And lying down upon the sandie graile,
   Drunke of the streame, as clear as cristall glas,
   Eftsoones his manly forces gan to faile . . . (VII.6)

The Knight succumbs to temptation. He falls, with Duessa. He is becoming less than 'man'.

6. The light whereof, that heaven's light did pas,
   Such blazing brightnesse through the aier threw,
   That eye mote not the same endure to vew. (VIII.19)

Arthur's shield, one of the many light images. It is linked to Una, also continually associated with light. The student might also reflect on the playing with 'mote', which means 'might', but also carries the suggestion of 'mote' as in the biblical sense of the mote in the eye.

7. A loathly, wrinckled hag, ill fauoured, old,
   Whose secret filth good manners biddeth not be told. (VIII.46)

Duessa revealed.

8. Why shouldst thou then despeire, that chosen art? (IX.53)

Una's encouragement to her Knight in despair.

9. . . . thee a Ploughman all unweeting fond . . . (X.66)

The Knight's origins—he was found by a ploughman, and is therefore called George, 'of the earth'. He is to become St George in Jerusalem.

10. [He] lay as in a dreame of deepe delight,
Besmeared with pretious Balme, whose vertuous might
Did heale his wounds . . . (XI.50)

The Knight under the Tree of Life on the second night of his contest with the Dragon.

11. The blazing brightnesse of her beauties beame,
And glorious light of her sunshyny face . . . (XII.23)

Una's brightness at the close, when she and her Knight are betrothed. Truth is clear and simple, like the sun's light in heaven.

Arrangement of material

In answering examination questions, it is useful to have three or four points to make about the question asked (there is no need for more); and you should draw the attention of the examiner to the fact that you do have three or four points to make. You should emphasise that your answer is not a continuous blur, and that you are in charge of your material.

Almost any question on Book I of *The Faerie Queene* will give you an opportunity to write about one or more of the following:

1. Spenser's intention.
2. His allegorical method.
3. The religious implications of his approach.
4. The biblical background.
5. His style.
6. His setting.
7. His use of contrasts.

You might also be able to bring in some of the historical background to the work, to show that you are confident in your knowledge of Spenser's work in its context.

Specimen questions

1. C. S. Lewis wrote: 'Spenser expected his readers to find in *The Faerie Queene* not his philosophy but their own experience—everyone's experience—loosened from its particular contexts by the universalising power of allegory.' Discuss.
2. Northrop Frye writes: 'The quest of the Red Crosse Knight in Book I follows the symbolism of the quest of Christ.' Discuss.

3. 'Arthur is the symbol of the ardour and strength of God's grace' (Martha Craig). Consider the role of Arthur in Book I of *The Faerie Queene*.
4. 'Spenser's art reflects his ideal of human perfectibility.' Discuss.
5. 'Throughout Book I of *The Faerie Queene* unity is continually parodied by doubleness.' Discuss.
6. How successful is Spenser in blending narrative, moral intention, and historical allegory in Book I of *The Faerie Queene*?
7. Consider the artistic effectiveness of Spenser's poetic language.

Specimen answer

Question 1: C. S. Lewis wrote: 'Spenser expected his readers to find in *The Faerie Queene* not his philosophy but their own experience—everyone's experience—loosened from its particular contexts by the universalising power of allegory.' Discuss.

Behind Spenser's writing there is the view that we live in a world which is fallen from grace. This fallen state is in evidence everywhere: in our dealings with others; in our prayers; even in our lack of self-respect. We are a race of beings who have gone astray and are wandering in a wood of confusion, difficulty, and sin. Arthur's comment as he rescues the Red Crosse Knight from the Castle of Orgoglio sums this up:

> This dayes ensample hath this lesson deare
> Deepe written in my heart with yron pen,
> That blisse may not abide in state of mortal men. (VIII.44)

Although the Red Crosse Knight is 'chosen' by Una (as the one to defeat the Dragon, and to free Eden from his dominance), as soon as he embarks on his quest with her, he goes astray in the wandering wood, which leads him into the Cave of Error. He is a Knight Errant: in other words, like all human beings, he is inclined to err.

This allegorical cave of Errour is *ours*, as Spenser makes wittily clear in the name he devises for this place of trial. The description he gives of this monster (who, as a serpent, is a forerunner of Orgoglio's beast and the Dragon, who controls Eden) is horrifying and gruesome, but she is a creature that is not unfamiliar to us by any means. In the allegory she is a perversion, or parody, of the natural: she gives shelter to her young, which is a perfectly normal thing to do, but in her case they actually climb back into her. And while it is a common idea that we gain sustenance from books, she feeds upon them, and spews them out when challenged. As always in Spenser, the ideas are very simple: we all know the type of person who chews up books and spews them out on every possible occasion, but in Spenser's allegorical visualisation we watch the monster actually doing this, thereby bringing the idea home to our minds. Spenser, through the universalising power of his allegory, makes us see in order to realise the nature of our experience.

The Red Crosse Knight, as the story proceeds, goes disastrously astray. He leaves the truth behind, and takes up with a semblance of it, all the time unaware of the real nature of Duessa. And when he hears the tale of Fradubio, whose name (doubt—the knight has doubted his lady) and story refer directly to his own condition, he remains unaware of this. How common this experience is hardly needs to be pointed out: we all know the state of lack of awareness, when we fail to see the obvious simply because we do not wish to see it, and we want to persist in the hazy doubleness that is comfortable and pleasurable.

The Red Crosse Knight continues with Duessa, falling more and more under her spell, until he truly falls. This is presented, not as a great, self-conscious act of deliberate evil, but as a much more insidious (and credible) business of going along with the general run of things. Duessa seems to be attractive, the day is pleasant, there is an agreeable fountain; why not lie down and take one's ease. He pays court to Duessa as he lies on the ground, 'pourd out in loosenesse'. The allegorical method, interpreting the situation as it proceeds, is making us aware ('pourd', 'loosenesse') that this dalliance, though seemingly pleasurable, is full of danger. Spenser actually says that the Knight is 'carelesse of his health'. While his armour is off, Orgoglio comes to take him over. And again, we can recognise what the allegory is trying to bring home to us from common experience: we submit, through laziness, inertia, or feebleness; and then, having given in, having surrendered our true selves, we are taken over by a false and domineering one, an Orgoglio of the self, in whose castle resides a monster, and where the 'dongeons' are unspeakably filthy and rotten.

So far, attention has been paid to the way in which Spenser emphasises the negative side of human nature, in the allegory. But he also depicts the positive. Una, for example, true to the name, remains faithful to her one Knight, and brings him to the House of Holinesse where he is made whole. The process of gaining Holinesse is represented through the physical discipline of healing in the allegory. The Knight is being made whole so he can face the Dragon.

Spenser's allegory presents our experiences—of trouble, difficulty, laziness, ignorance, inertia; and of joy, delight, awareness and peace—in highly visual ways, so that they may enter into the reader's mind to be understood and apprehended as part of his moral nature. Spenser wants his allegory to make his reader more aware and more disciplined, because more fully conscious of the struggle for the possession of the soul going on at every moment of life.

Suggested outlines for other answers

Question 4: Spenser's art reflects his ideal of human perfectibility. Discuss.

(i) Spenser's ideal of 'fashioning a gentleman' through his art
(ii) Vision of Jerusalem which is given to the Red Crosse Knight
(iii) How he is to get there—his trials (Duessa, Despair)
grace (Arthur)
Holiness (Wholenesse)
the defeat of the Dragon
betrothal to Una
(iv) Spenser's verse technique as a method for developing greater insight and coherence

Question 7: Consider the artistic effectiveness of Spenser's poetic language.

(i) Archaism of Spenser's language
(ii) Its Englishness (Chaucer)
(iii) It allows more word-play which makes the reader conscious of how he can come to understand what is beyond the obvious
(iv) Discipline of his verse
(v) His verse can enact a process of realisation

Part 5

Suggestions for further reading

The text

An invaluable new edition, to which these notes are heavily indebted, is *The Faerie Queene*, edited by A. C. Hamilton, in the Annotated English Poets Series, Longman, London and New York, 1977. This is of immense help to the student because a commentary is printed alongside the text, in which much of the modern and traditional critical discussion of Spenser's work is summarised around specific points as these present themselves in the poem. The general introduction to this edition outlines the main branches of criticism which the work has stimulated, while the introduction to Book I summarises the main lines of interpretation.

The standard edition, and the one from which many students will find themselves working, is *The Poetical Works of Edmund Spenser*, edited by J. C. Smith and Ernest de Selincourt, Oxford University Press, Oxford, 1912; issued in paperback, 1970. The print is very small and it contains no commentary, but the glossary at the back is useful.

A Penguin edition of *The Faerie Queene* was edited by Thomas P. Roche, Jr. and C. Patrick O'Donnell, Jr., Penguin Books, Harmondsworth, 1978. This volume is unwieldy, though there are some useful notes at the back.

Biography

The standard life of Spenser is that by Alexander C. Judson, *The Life of Edmund Spenser*, Volume 10 of the Variorum edition of *The Works of Edmund Spenser*, edited by Edwin Greenlaw and others, Johns Hopkins Press, Baltimore, 1932-49. (Volume 10 appeared in 1945.)

Criticism

ALPERS, PAUL J. (ED.): *Edmund Spenser: A Critical Anthology*, Penguin Books, Harmondsworth, 1969. A useful compilation, containing criticism and comment, from Spenser's own day up to fairly recent times. See especially the essays by Martha Craig, 'The Secret Wit of Spenser's Language' and by Northrop Frye, 'The Structure of Imagery in *The Faerie Queene*'.

FOWLER, ALASTAIR: *Spenser and the Numbers of Time*, Routledge, London, 1964. An examination of the numerological and astronomical patterns of *The Faerie Queene*. Discusses the 'oneness' of Una and her link with the sun.

HAMILTON, A. C.: *The Structure of the Allegory in 'The Faerie Queene'*, Clarendon Press, Oxford, 1961. This examines the evolution of the allegorical meaning in terms of the growth of Christian understanding.

LEWIS, C. S.: *The Allegory of Love*, Oxford University Press, Oxford, 1936. The last chapter is a seminal study of Spenser's meanings and how he conveys them.

MACCAFFREY, ISOBEL G.: *Spenser's Allegory*, Princeton University Press, Princeton, 1976. This lays emphasis on the involvement of the reader in the deciphering of the meanings of the allegory.

NELSON, WILLIAM: *The Poetry of Spenser*, Columbia University Press, New York, 1963. This examines the theme of renewal in Book I.

NOHRNBERG, JAMES: *The Analogy of 'The Faerie Queene'*, Princeton University Press, Princeton, 1976. This provides an extensive commentary on the poem's meaning. A mammoth work of criticism and scholarship.

O'CONNELL, MICHAEL: *Mirror and Veil*, University of North Carolina Press, Chapel Hill, 1977. This discusses the historical dimension of *The Faerie Queene*.

RENWICK, W. L.: *Edmund Spenser*, Edward Arnold, London, 1925. A readable, entertaining, and by no means outdated study of Spenser.

WILLIAMS, KATHLEEN: *Spenser's Faerie Queene: The World of Glass*, University of California Press, Berkeley, 1966. This emphasises the relationship between Spenser's poem and the experience of living.

Background reading

BINDOFF, S. T.: *Tudor England*, Penguin Books, Harmondsworth, 1966.

GREEN, J. R.: *A Short History of the English People*, Macmillan, London, 1876.

WILLIAMS, NEVILLE: *Elizabeth, Queen of England*, Weidenfeld and Nicolson, London, 1967.

The author of these notes

ROBERT WELCH is a graduate of University College, Cork, and of the University of Leeds. He was a lecturer at the University of Ife, Nigeria, before taking up his present post as Lecturer in English literature at the University of Leeds. He has published articles on Irish literature, and on Victorian and modern literature. He is the author of *Irish Poetry from Moore to Yeats* (1980); he has edited a volume of essays on George Moore, *The Way Back* (1982); and is at work on a *Companion to Irish Literature*. He has written York Notes on George Orwell's *Animal Farm* and *1984*.

YORK NOTES

The first 200 titles

	Series number
CHINUA ACHEBE	
A Man of the People	(116)
Arrow of God	(92)
Things Fall Apart	(96)
ELECHI AMADI	
The Concubine	(139)
JOHN ARDEN	
Serjeant Musgrave's Dance	(159)
AYI KWEI ARMAH	
The Beautyful Ones Are Not Yet Born	(154)
JANE AUSTEN	
Emma	(142)
Northanger Abbey	(1)
Persuasion	(69)
Pride and Prejudice	(62)
Sense and Sensibility	(91)
SAMUEL BECKETT	
Waiting for Godot	(115)
SAUL BELLOW	
Henderson, The Rain King	(146)
ARNOLD BENNETT	
Anna of the Five Towns	(144)
WILLIAM BLAKE	
Songs of Innocence, Songs of Experience	(173)
ROBERT BOLT	
A Man For All Seasons	(51)
CHARLOTTE BRONTË	
Jane Eyre	(21)
EMILY BRONTË	
Wuthering Heights	(43)
JOHN BUCHAN	
The Thirty-Nine Steps	(89)
ALBERT CAMUS	
L'Etranger (The Outsider)	(46)
GEOFFREY CHAUCER	
Prologue to the Canterbury Tales	(30)
The Franklin's Tale	(78)
The Knight's Tale	(97)
The Merchant's Tale	(193)
The Miller's Tale	(192)
The Nun's Priest's Tale	(16)
The Pardoner's Tale	(50)
The Wife of Bath's Tale	(109)
Troilus and Criseyde	(198)
SAMUEL TAYLOR COLERIDGE	
Selected Poems	(165)
WILKIE COLLINS	
The Woman in White	(182)
SIR ARTHUR CONAN DOYLE	
The Hound of the Baskervilles	(53)
JOSEPH CONRAD	
Heart of Darkness	(152)
Lord Jim	(150)
Nostromo	(68)
The Secret Agent	(138)
Youth and *Typhoon*	(100)
DANIEL DEFOE	
Moll Flanders	(153)
Robinson Crusoe	(28)
CHARLES DICKENS	
A Tale of Two Cities	(70)
Bleak House	(183)
David Copperfield	(9)
Great Expectations	(66)
Nicholas Nickleby	(161)
Oliver Twist	(101)
The Pickwick Papers	(110)
JOHN DONNE	
Selected Poems	(199)
THEODORE DREISER	
Sister Carrie	(179)
GEORGE ELIOT	
Adam Bede	(14)
Silas Marner	(98)
The Mill on the Floss	(29)
T. S. ELIOT	
Four Quartets	(167)
Murder in the Cathedral	(149)
Selected Poems	(155)
The Waste Land	(45)
WILLIAM FAULKNER	
Absalom, Absalom!	(124)
As I Lay Dying	(44)
Go Down, Moses	(163)
The Sound and the Fury	(136)
HENRY FIELDING	
Joseph Andrews	(105)
Tom Jones	(113)
F. SCOTT FITZGERALD	
The Great Gatsby	(8)
E. M. FORSTER	
A Passage to India	(151)
ATHOL FUGARD	
Selected Plays	(63)
MRS GASKELL	
North and South	(60)
WILLIAM GOLDING	
Lord of the Flies	(77)
OLIVER GOLDSMITH	
She Stoops to Conquer	(71)
The Vicar of Wakefield	(79)
GRAHAM GREENE	
The Power and the Glory	(188)
THOMAS HARDY	
Far From the Madding Crowd	(174)
Jude the Obscure	(6)
Selected Poems	(169)
Tess of the D'Urbervilles	(80)
The Mayor of Casterbridge	(39)
The Return of the Native	(20)
The Trumpet Major	(74)
The Woodlanders	(160)
Under the Greenwood Tree	(129)
L. P. HARTLEY	
The Go-Between	(36)
The Shrimp and the Anemone	(123)
NATHANIEL HAWTHORNE	
The Scarlet Letter	(134)
ERNEST HEMINGWAY	
A Farewell to Arms	(145)
For Whom the Bell Tolls	(95)
The Old Man and the Sea	(11)
HERMANN HESSE	
Steppenwolf	(135)
BARRY HINES	
Kes	(189)
ANTHONY HOPE	
The Prisoner of Zenda	(88)
WILLIAM DEAN HOWELLS	
The Rise of Silas Lapham	(175)
RICHARD HUGHES	
A High Wind in Jamaica	(17)
THOMAS HUGHES	
Tom Brown's Schooldays	(2)

	Series number
ALDOUS HUXLEY	
Brave New World	(156)
HENRIK IBSEN	
A Doll's House	(85)
Ghosts	(131)
HENRY JAMES	
Daisy Miller	(147)
The Europeans	(120)
The Portrait of a Lady	(117)
The Turn of the Screw	(27)
SAMUEL JOHNSON	
Rasselas	(137)
BEN JONSON	
The Alchemist	(102)
Volpone	(15)
RUDYARD KIPLING	
Kim	(114)
D. H. LAWRENCE	
Sons and Lovers	(24)
The Rainbow	(59)
Women in Love	(143)
CAMARA LAYE	
L'Enfant Noir	(191)
HARPER LEE	
To Kill a Mocking-Bird	(125)
LAURIE LEE	
Cider with Rosie	(186)
THOMAS MANN	
Tonio Kröger	(168)
CHRISTOPHER MARLOWE	
Doctor Faustus	(127)
Edward II	(166)
W. SOMERSET MAUGHAM	
Of Human Bondage	(185)
Selected Short Stories	(38)
HERMAN MELVILLE	
Billy Budd	(10)
Moby Dick	(126)
ARTHUR MILLER	
Death of a Salesman	(32)
The Crucible	(3)
JOHN MILTON	
Paradise Lost I & II	(94)
Paradise Lost IV & IX	(87)
Selected Poems	(177)
V. S. NAIPAUL	
A House for Mr Biswas	(180)
SEAN O'CASEY	
Juno and the Paycock	(112)
The Shadow of a Gunman	(200)
GABRIEL OKARA	
The Voice	(157)
EUGENE O'NEILL	
Mourning Becomes Electra	(130)
GEORGE ORWELL	
Animal Farm	(37)
Nineteen Eighty-four	(67)
JOHN OSBORNE	
Look Back in Anger	(128)
HAROLD PINTER	
The Birthday Party	(25)
The Caretaker	(106)
ALEXANDER POPE	
Selected Poems	(194)
THOMAS PYNCHON	
The Crying of Lot 49	(148)
SIR WALTER SCOTT	
Ivanhoe	(58)
Quentin Durward	(54)
The Heart of Midlothian	(141)
Waverley	(122)
PETER SHAFFER	
The Royal Hunt of the Sun	(170)
WILLIAM SHAKESPEARE	
A Midsummer Night's Dream	(26)
Antony and Cleopatra	(82)
As You Like It	(108)
Coriolanus	(35)
Cymbeline	(93)

	Series number
Hamlet	(84)
Henry IV Part I	(83)
Henry IV Part II	(140)
Henry V	(40)
Julius Caesar	(13)
King Lear	(18)
Love's Labour's Lost	(72)
Macbeth	(4)
Measure for Measure	(33)
Much Ado About Nothing	(73)
Othello	(34)
Richard II	(41)
Richard III	(119)
Romeo and Juliet	(64)
Sonnets	(181)
The Merchant of Venice	(107)
The Taming of the Shrew	(118)
The Tempest	(22)
The Winter's Tale	(65)
Troilus and Cressida	(47)
Twelfth Night	(42)
GEORGE BERNARD SHAW	
Androcles and the Lion	(56)
Arms and the Man	(12)
Caesar and Cleopatra	(57)
Major Barbara	(195)
Pygmalion	(5)
RICHARD BRINSLEY SHERIDAN	
The School for Scandal	(55)
The Rivals	(104)
WOLE SOYINKA	
The Lion and the Jewel	(158)
The Road	(133)
Three Short Plays	(172)
JOHN STEINBECK	
Of Mice and Men	(23)
The Grapes of Wrath	(7)
The Pearl	(99)
ROBERT LOUIS STEVENSON	
Kidnapped	(90)
Treasure Island	(48)
Dr Jekyll and Mr Hyde	(132)
JONATHAN SWIFT	
Gulliver's Travels	(61)
JOHN MILLINGTON SYNGE	
The Playboy of the Western World	(111)
W. M. THACKERAY	
Vanity Fair	(19)
DYLAN THOMAS	
Under Milk Wood	(197)
J. R. R. TOLKIEN	
The Hobbit	(121)
MARK TWAIN	
Huckleberry Finn	(49)
Tom Sawyer	(76)
VOLTAIRE	
Candide	(81)
EVELYN WAUGH	
Decline and Fall	(178)
JOHN WEBSTER	
The Duchess of Malfi	(171)
The White Devil	(176)
H. G. WELLS	
The History of Mr Polly	(86)
The Invisible Man	(52)
The War of the Worlds	(103)
ARNOLD WESKER	
Chips with Everything	(184)
Roots	(164)
PATRICK WHITE	
Voss	(190)
OSCAR WILDE	
The Importance of Being Earnest	(75)
TENNESSEE WILLIAMS	
The Glass Menagerie	(187)
VIRGINIA WOOLF	
To the Lighthouse	(162)
WILLIAM WORDSWORTH	
Selected Poems	(196)